MW00785184

LEGENDARY LOCALS

OF

AMELIA ISLAND

FLORIDA

Fernandina, 1884

This print from 1884 is a detailed view of Fernandina as it stood at that time. J.J. Stoner, who was based in Madison, Wisconsin, drew it; he traveled the country drawing similar illustrations of cities and then offered them for sale. This illustration of Amelia Island was completed at the height of Fernandina's prominence on the Eastern Seaboard. (Courtesy Hicks family collection.)

Page 1: Lynn Joyner and His Record Fish

Lynn Joyner stands next to his record-breaking goliath grouper. Joyner was just a sophomore in high school on May 20, 1961, when he caught the fish off the "ice dock," located approximately where the Port of Fernandina Beach is today. A tow truck was used to pull the fish ashore, and scales from one of the paper mills were used to weigh it. The fish measured seven feet, one and a half inches long, and weighed 680 pounds. This remains the record catch for the species. (Courtesy Amelia Island Museum of History.)

LEGENDARY LOCALS

— OF —

AMELIA ISLAND

FLORIDA

ROB HICKS

LEGENDARY
LOCALS

Copyright © 2017 by Rob Hicks
ISBN 9781540216540

Legendary Locals is an imprint of Arcadia Publishing
Charleston, South Carolina

Library of Congress Control Number: 2016960257

For all general information, please contact Arcadia Publishing:
Telephone 843-853-2070
Fax 843-853-0044
E-mail sales@arcadiapublishing.com
For customer service and orders:
Toll-Free 1-888-313-2665

Visit us on the Internet at www.arcadiapublishing.com

On the Front Cover: Clockwise from top left:
William Burbank Sr. and sons, net makers (courtesy Amelia Island Museum of History; see page 54), MaVynee Betsch, activist (courtesy Amelia Island Museum of History; see page 105), Chris Bryan, entrepreneur (author's collection; see page 96), Stephan "Steve" Leimberg, law professor and photographer (courtesy Steve Leimberg/UnSeenImages.com; see page 123), Mary Duffy, educator and sea turtle watch organizer (author's collection; see page 90), Gregor MacGregor, political con artist (courtesy Florida State Archives; see page 19), Steve Colwell, confectioner (author's collection; see page 109), Felix Jones, local icon (author's collection; see page 87), Joseph Finnegan, general and railroad attorney (courtesy Florida State Archives; see page 25).

On the Back Cover: From left to right:
Isle of Eight Flags Shrimp Festival founder Melvin Dougherty (center) and Fernandina Beach's first female city commissioner, Grace Butler (second from right) (courtesy City of Fernandina Beach Archives; see pages 67 and 82), Ron Sapp, educator and city commissioner (author's collection; see page 80).

CONTENTS

ACKNOWLEDGMENTS

Writing this book was a vastly different experience than that of my others. With those, the narrative was mostly guided by the historical pictures available. In the case of this book, the narrative did not start with the photographs. It began with a list of people who I felt were the key contributors to Amelia's earliest recorded days and the "eight-flag" history. From there, I assembled a list of the people who were impactful through their local leadership and influence. They are the individuals who not only physically built our historic downtown and community, but also possessed the wisdom to preserve its prosperity. The latter part of the book explores the members of this community today.

It was never my intent for this book to be a hall of fame (though I do chair the Fernandina Beach High School Hall of Fame Committee). Instead, I wanted to highlight individuals who I felt were representative of all the different facets of society and business that comprise our community. So, it was with such a list of some 200 people that I set to bring this book to publication.

Assembling the stories of those 200 people and their photographs could not have happened without the help of some key individuals. My good friend Ron Sapp holds a wealth of knowledge of Fernandina's political history and provided much more insight than there is print space. Others, like the late Mary Agnes Wolff White, helped provide color, connect the branches of family trees, and offered their own perspectives. As far as the photographs, no one was as valuable as Steve Leimberg. Steve is perhaps the most talented Amelia Island resident, and I am so fortunate to have his permission to use many of his amazing portraits here. More of his work can be seen on his website UnseenImages.com. I should also thank the Amelia Island Museum of History and the countless people in this book and their family and friends who I hounded for photographs. Thanks for being patient.

Finally, I should thank my children and wife, Kim, who served as a sounding board and as my assistant in so many ways along the way. A legendary local in her own right—I appreciate all you do!

INTRODUCTION

Amelia Island has some distinguishing characteristics. It is roughly 13 miles long and about 2 miles wide at its widest point, which are about the same dimensions of Manhattan Island. It lies at the northeastern-most corner of Florida. From the north end, one can see Georgia's Cumberland Island just a couple of hundred yards away—a view that once looked across an international border. The two islands mark the westernmost point of the Atlantic Ocean, which offers considerable protection from hurricanes. This fact, along with the naturally deep surrounding waters, means there was no coincidence in the US Navy's decision to build a submarine base nearby. Amelia is home to an abundance of natural springs that quenched the thirst of its earliest residents. The springs are lesser known today as the utilities services that tap into them keep their levels low. There are bluffs and ancient dunes that provide varied topography from which sprawling oak trees and towering pine trees grow. These trees give way to wide beaches that were used as runways for airplanes and raceways for drag racers before hotels and condominiums were built by the tourism industry.

These unique features have conspired to bring a wealth of diverse people to Amelia Island. To the earliest people, the Timucuan Indians, the island was simply a habitable place. There was freshwater to drink, fertile soil to plant in, an abundance of land to settle, and marine animals to eat. The French and Spanish brought European religions to Amelia Island. The Spanish established missions to the natives. For this, they chose a small neck of land on a short bluff on the island's west side. Today, we call this Old Town.

Politics became involved. The island flip-flopped between Spanish and English control, which brought people with varied interests and melded a population of two nations. When the English finally left the region, Florida remained in Spain's possession. Amelia formed the border with the newly formed United States including Georgia to the north. The Spanish, however, did not provide enough resources to effectively maintain control of the island. Meanwhile, Thomas Jefferson had enacted the Embargo Act, which forbade the United States from trading with foreign entities. For a loosely controlled border town, this meant incredible, if nefarious, opportunity.

People of all sorts and nationalities came to Amelia at this time. Some claimed the island as their own and raised their own flags. Others just used Amelia Island and its winding marshy waterways to elude officials as they smuggled illegal goods into the United States.

In time, Amelia came into the possession of the United States. This meant more new people. Following the Civil War, a railroad was constructed across the state that connected the Atlantic Ocean at Amelia Island with the Gulf of Mexico at Cedar Key. This shortcut around the peninsula meant another explosion of the local economy. People who might have visited the island during the Civil War returned with their families and were hired by the railroad or shipping companies. The port bustled as so much of Florida's rich lumber reserves were shipped from Amelia Island.

When shipping lumber was expanded in other areas and fell off locally, Amelia Island recruited paper mills to fill the economic void. They found the preestablished infrastructure for getting lumber to the island and the ability to draw from the Amelia River conducive to their operations. Around the turn of the 20th century, the waters of Amelia Island teemed with marine life, including shrimp. The people who came to catch the shrimp brought their innovative ideas, and together, they revolutionized the shrimping industry forever. The mills and fruitful waters brought more people still, and the island became a blue-collar community.

Jacksonville was changing during this time too, and much of the focus on Northeast Florida shifted there. That meant cheaper land remained on Amelia Island, especially at the south end where there was already a small African American community. From this, a black resort community, known as American Beach, sprang. Amelia Island became a haven for blacks who had longed for a vacation destination to call their own amidst Jim Crow laws. While Amelia Island had already been host to scores of remarkable African Americans, American Beach promised a continuation of a tradition of black historical significance.

By the 1970s, there was no doubt Florida was a hotbed for tourism. Amelia's beaches were selected for the construction of new resorts. Jacksonville's nearby airport, the convergence of two major interstates in Interstate 95 and Interstate 10, and the opportunity to get into Florida without having to drive all the way down the state positioned the island nicely as it entered this market on a larger stage. More hotels and restaurants were built, which begot more tourists, hotels, and restaurants, in that order. The quality of these restaurants and resorts gave Amelia Island a more luxurious appeal than many other places. Individuals who had made fortunes elsewhere visited Amelia on vacation and realized the splendors of this little island with its majestic beaches and beautiful marshes. They have retired here, and these talented people have integrated themselves into the fabric of local society.

Today, there are still shrimpers with deep roots here. African Americans still have their vacation homes at American Beach. The mills and shipping from the Port of Fernandina are essential to the local economy. The resorts at the south end of the island bring visitors from all over the world while others drive in from areas close by just to spend the day. Many of the visitors fall in love with Amelia and eventually make it their home. What this means is that this place is home to a complex community filled with remarkable people. Their activities here are varied, but they share a common bond in that it was the island itself, the unique piece of land and its features, that originally drew them here.

CHAPTER ONE

The Island
Becomes Amelia

The Timucuan Indians were the first people to inhabit Amelia Island, which they called Napoyca. They spoke their own language and comprised about 35 chiefdoms that spread throughout Northeast and North Central Florida. They lived on Amelia as early as 2,500 BCE and had several settlements around the island. The natives hunted animals like deer and alligators and cultivated the land with crops such as corn, beans, and squash. The Timucuans had a healthy appetite for seafood including oysters, which they harvested from the marshy areas surrounding the island. They dropped oyster shells on the spot as they ate them, and over the years, these mounds of shells grew quite large. These mounds remain today in some places and are called middens.

The Timucuans' appearance was a sight to behold. They earned tattoos through various deeds and acts. Those with higher social status may have been completely covered, even on their lips, with elaborate markings made by cutting the skin with shells and applying berry juice or ash. They made jewelry and accessories from bones and shells and traded for other items with tribes from other areas. Another notable feature was their hair. The Timucuans grew their hair long and then wound it up into a conical shape on their heads; Feathers or other decorations were often added. This gave an appearance of increased height, which led the first (and shorter) Europeans who encountered them to describe the natives as over seven feet tall. Timucuan skeletons average a height of about five feet, ten inches.

Some of those early encounters between the Europeans and Timucuans took place on Amelia Island. Eventually, the Spanish established missions to them. The first mission on Amelia, Santa Maria, was established in 1573 near present-day Old Town. It would eventually be replaced by the Santa Catalina de Guale Mission when a number of other natives were relocated to the island from Georgia.

Amelia Island can hold its own against better-known locales in New World history. While the Timucuans were the first to settle here, the Europeans' arrival marked the beginning of the claim by eight different sovereign states to the island. Indeed, by 1861, Amelia Island had earned its nickname, the Isle of Eight Flags, as the only place in America to lay under so many standards. This chapter explores the most influential people who contributed to the political flux under those early flags.

Jean Ribault

Jean Ribault was the first European to land on the island. He did so in early May 1562 and called Amelia "Isle de Mai." Ribault met the Timucuan Indians and later wrote about that encounter, apparently impressed with their agricultural capabilities. His mission was officially sponsored by France, which aimed to establish a Protestant colony in Florida. Ribault further explored the coast, and eventually returned to Europe. Upon seeking additional supplies in England, he was arrested and imprisoned for threatening Spanish interests already established in Florida, as King Philip II of Spain was married to Queen Elizabeth of England's sister. (Courtesy Florida State Archives.)

René Laudonniere

René Laudonniere was second in command to Ribault on his voyage to Florida. After Ribault's imprisonment, Laudonniere was sent back to Florida and established Fort Caroline on the banks of the St. Johns River on the north side of what is now Jacksonville. This placed the area, including Amelia Island, under French rule. (Courtesy Florida State Archives.)

Pedro Menéndez

The Spanish had been the first Europeans to land in Florida, which they did in 1513 under Ponce de León. For the next 50 years, they continued to explore the New World and made several attempts to establish settlements in Florida. They all failed, and Spain made an official decree in 1561 that they were abandoning attempts to settle the peninsula. They did not, however, give up their claim to the land since they had been the ones who discovered it.

The French saw that decree as their opportunity to get their foothold in the New World, and that was a motivating factor in Ribault's initial expedition. Of course, his miscalculation of Queen Elizabeth alerted the Spanish to France's intent and squarely placed France and Spain at odds over the Florida peninsula.

Pedro Menéndez de Aviles, pictured here, was an admiral in the Spanish Navy. Before the French came to Florida, Menéndez had already been planning to search for a route that connected the Atlantic and Pacific Oceans. The Spanish monarchy gave him jurisdiction over the whole east coast of North America in which to do so. Once Fort Caroline was established, Menéndez's mission was amended to include dealing with that problem, as the Spanish saw it. Spaniards feared French ships from Fort Caroline would be in prime position to attack Spanish ships returning to Spain from South America and the Caribbean full of treasure and goods.

By 1565, Ribault had been released from prison and set off to return to Florida in order to strengthen the Fort Caroline settlement, which had been struggling due to a food shortage. Menéndez knew of Ribault's plans and established St. Augustine as the base of defense against the French. The stage was set for the showdown between Ribault and Menéndez.

The French struck first as they sailed south to St. Augustine from Fort Caroline. A storm overtook the French ships though, and their soldiers were forced to land at an inlet south of the Spanish settlement. Realizing the majority of the French forces were languishing to his south, Menéndez seized the opportunity and marched his troops north to Fort Caroline. The Spanish overtook the fort with ease and killed all but the women and children. His army then pursued the French soldiers stranded to St. Augustine's south and ordered that they all be executed, including Ribault. Today, the inlet were the French met their demise is called Matanzas, the Spanish word for slaughter.

This brought French interests in Florida and Amelia Island firmly to an end. St. Augustine proved to finally be a successful endeavor for the Spanish in Florida, and the missions on Amelia Island were eventually established. (Courtesy Florida State Archives.)

11

James Oglethorpe
In 1732, Georgia was established as a British colony under the direction of James Oglethorpe. The southern border of Georgia was vague, and Amelia Island spent nearly 30 awkward years as a sort of buffer between Spanish Florida and British Georgia. However, the 1763 Treaty of Paris that ended the French and Indian War placed Amelia firmly in British hands. (Courtesy Florida State Archives.)

John Percival
John Percival, the Second Earl of Egmont, was granted most of Amelia Island, and it became known as the Isle of Egmont. It is unlikely that Percival ever visited the island himself. The 1783 Treaty of Paris ended the Revolutionary War, and Amelia Island was returned to Spain as it had supported the Patriots. (Courtesy Florida State Archives.)

Daniel McGirtt

The shift from British to Spanish control left the British settlers on the island in a bad situation. They could either change their allegiance to Spain or leave the island within 18 months. Most of those who left, which was the majority, went to either the Caribbean or Nova Scotia.

Originally from South Carolina, Daniel McGirtt ended up in North Florida and southern Georgia and was the leader of a group called the banditti; they preyed on the destitute British loyalists who suddenly found themselves in Spanish territory. The banditti terrorized Amelia Island and the surrounding areas and took whatever they wanted from British homesteads, including livestock, slaves, and personal treasures. (Courtesy Florida State Archives.)

Stephen Egan

Stephen Egan served as John Percival's superintendent and oversaw an indigo plantation on the Earl's behalf. The blue dye derived from indigo had become a popular status symbol in England. Egan was initially sent to St. Augustine to learn how to farm indigo and convert it to a useful product. Once on Amelia, he was known for his kind treatment of slaves, including allowing them to marry each other and have families. He even let slaves act as tradesmen among themselves. At some point during his tenure, the long creek that runs down the center of the island acquired Egan's name. This photograph looks north at the creek from Atlantic Avenue. (Author's collection.)

13

Col. Samuel Elbert

There was one incident related to the Revolutionary War on the island. Col. Samuel Elbert of the Continental Army landed a small group of soldiers on the British-controlled Island in 1777. One of those soldiers was promptly killed by the opposition. In retribution, Colonel Elbert and his men proceeded to burn every house on the defenseless island. (Courtesy County of Elberton, Georgia.)

John Vaughan

John Vaughan was a Revolutionary War soldier who served under Gen. George Washington. His military service later brought him to Georgia, and from there, he eventually acquired 250 acres on Amelia Island through a Spanish land grant. Vaughan established a cotton plantation called Old Nest near present-day Amelia City. Records are unclear, but Vaughan may have acquired as many as 1,000 more acres on the island at one point and owned as many as 500 slaves. He is buried beneath this obelisk in a small cemetery at the south end of the island. (Author's collection.)

George Clarke

George Clarke was British by birth but became a Spanish loyalist. He moved to Amelia Island in 1808 with his wife, a freed slave. The Spanish made him the surveyor general of East Florida in 1811, and his knowledge of the area was unsurpassed.

Clarke was an extraordinarily active citizen on the island and had the ear of the governor. It was Clarke who named the town on Amelia Island Fernandina after Ferdinand VII of Spain and platted the town at what is now Old Town. He moved to St. Marys, Georgia, in 1817, at the peak of Amelia's political tumult, but continued to be influential in East Florida until his death sometime in the mid-1830s. His original plat of Old Town is seen here. (Courtesy Florida State Archives.)

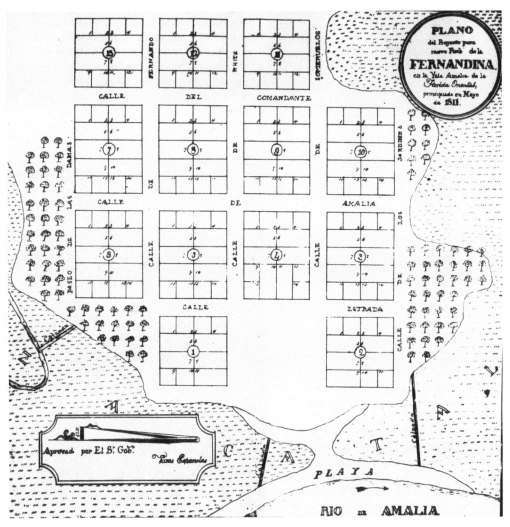

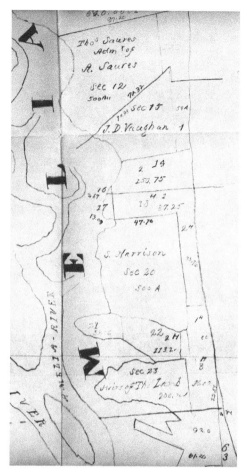

Samuel Harrison

Samuel Harrison brought his family to Amelia in the early 1790s and obtained a Spanish land grant. While most of the previous activity here happened at what is now present-day Old Town, the Harrisons lived at the south end of the island along Harrison Creek at what is now part of the Omni Amelia Island Plantation Resort. Harrison owned many slaves who worked his plantations and grew things like indigo and sea island cotton. When Union forces occupied the island during the Civil War, the family burned their home so soldiers would not take it over. After the war, they rebuilt. This early map shows the location of Harrison's plantation as well as the plantation of John Vaughan. (Courtesy Amelia Island Museum of History.)

Jimmy Drummond

"Uncle" Jimmy Drummond often worked around Harrison's old plantation but lived in a shack near where the entrance to Fort Clinch State Park is today. He came from the Everglades with a few other Seminole Indians in 1846. He claimed to be a Native American, but many supposed he was black. Drummond trained snakes and was revered in the local black community as a conjurer. White locals and visitors to the island often came to see him and to listen to his fantastic stories, like the one about the treasure buried under a tree marked with a chain somewhere on the island. Drummond died in 1933 at the age of 107. This photograph was taken from an early newspaper. (Courtesy Amelia Island Museum of History.)

Ferdinand VII

Ferdinand VII was hardly a local, but since the town bears his name, he is worth discussing. He ascended to the Spanish throne in March 1808 but was very quickly overthrown by Napoleon in less than two months' time. His kingship was returned in late 1813 and he held it until his death in 1833.

In general, Fernandina Beach should take little pride in bearing this king's name. Historians do not hold him in high regard, nor did his subjects. It is interesting therefore that George Clarke chose to name the town after him, especially considering the fact that the town was platted between his two reigns, the first having lasted just 10 days. Perhaps he did so because at the time, Ferdinand was simply the last true Spanish king. The present king then was a Frenchman, Napoleon's brother Joseph. (Courtesy Amelia Island Museum of History.)

Princess Amelia of Great Britain

Fernandina Beach is the city upon the island of Amelia. The island held previous names, but after exploring it, George Oglethorpe named it after the second daughter of King George II. Princess Amelia never married but lived the typical life of a royal in London until her death in 1786. (Courtesy Amelia Island Museum of History.)

George Mathews

By 1811, Spanish-controlled Amelia Island was in turmoil as it served as a base for smuggling goods into Georgia and the United States, operating under the Non-Intercourse Act, which had replaced the Embargo Act. American general George Mathews was put in charge of a secret plan to use Floridians to rebel and seize the island, then turn it over to the United States, which would then have full control over the strategic port. Mathews is depicted at the far left of this painting of the Battle of Brandywine by artist Howard Pyle. (Courtesy Brandywine River Museum.)

John McIntosh

John McIntosh, a local planter, agreed to execute the plan in exchange for the promise of new land. McIntosh attracted 200 men who overtook the sparse Spanish resistance and raised the "patriot flag" over the island, calling it the Republic of Florida. McIntosh gave the island to America a day later per his deal with Mathews, but his patriots continued their assault on the Spanish and attacked St. Augustine. This angered Pres. James Madison. For diplomatic reasons, Madison was forced to return Amelia Island to the Spanish. (Courtesy Amelia Island Museum of History.)

Gregor MacGregor

Gregor MacGregor must be one of the most notorious con artists in all of history. He fabricated a rich nation called Poyais in Central America and advertised its opportunities in London. He sold land in this fake nation to British investors and sailed nearly 300 of them across the Atlantic. Once there, MacGregor dropped his patsies off in the untamed Central American jungle and essentially left them there to die.

Prior to that, MacGregor had tried his hand at creating nations on Amelia Island. He aimed to drive the Spanish out of Florida. He planned to take Amelia Island and use it as a base to capture the rest of the peninsula. In early 1817, MacGregor made the rounds of American cities gathering support for his cause. By the time he got to Savannah, he had two schooners, 150 men, and $30,000.

Amelia Island at the time was defended by 54 Spanish soldiers stationed at Fort San Carlos, which has since been lost to the Amelia River at Old Town. Some of MacGregor's supporters had started a rumor that he had 1,000 men, though that number had actually dwindled to 55. On June 29, he set siege on Amelia as the small militia crossed the sound from Cumberland and landed on the island. They proceeded to march through the forested area that is now Fort Clinch State Park. In doing so, they were plagued by mosquitoes, and the men cut sprigs of dog fennel, a natural insect repellent, to place in their hats. As the soldiers crossed Egans Creek they came in view of the Spanish at Fort San Carlos. The Spanish mistook the dog fennel as feathers, a sign of officers. They assumed that if there were 55 officers advancing, the rumors of a 1,000-man army must have been true. The Spanish surrendered the fort without a fight, and the island belonged to MacGregor.

Instead of pursuing the Spanish in the rest of Florida, MacGregor proceeded to live lavishly on Amelia. He raised the Green Cross of the Republic of Florida, printed his own money, and threw extravagant dinner parties. In short time, the people of Amelia came to realize there was little substance behind their new leader. (Courtesy Florida State Archives.)

Ruggles Hubbard and Jared Irwin

There are no heroes of Amelia Island's early history who are as unsung as Ruggles Hubbard and Jared Irwin. As the summer of 1817 stretched on and MacGregor's welcome on the island became increasingly overstayed, Hubbard and Irwin arrived. Hubbard had served as sheriff of New York before he arrived. Irwin was a Georgia native and member of the Pennsylvania House of Representatives. The men brought no money to settle MacGregor's debts, which is what was most needed, but they did provide leadership.

That leadership was particularly evident in the battle that took place on McClure's Hill. On September 4, MacGregor had realized his operations on Amelia Island had failed and abandoned the island. This essentially left the town in the hands of Hubbard and Irwin. Spanish loyalist George Clarke had kept Spanish authorities in St. Augustine abreast of the ongoing situation. Sensing increasing weakness, the Spanish planned to attack the island and reclaim it. On September 13, they attacked Fort San Carlos at Old Town from McClure's Hill, a rise in the land now on North Fourteenth Street and within a few hundred yards from the fort's location. The Spanish also placed gunboats in the harbor and began bombarding the fort from those. Artillery on the hill opposite the gunboats also fired upon the fort. Behind the hill, 200 soldiers supporting the Spanish sat in waiting, thinking themselves safe from the battle above their position.

Hubbard and Irwin worked feverishly inside Fort San Carlos organizing a defense of the island. As they fired at the guns on the hill, they overshot their target and landed cannonballs in the midst of the soldiers hiding behind it. Two men were killed, several more injured, and the rest of the forces panicked. The Spanish retreated from the hill, and the gunboats followed suit. Hubbard and Irwin had successfully defended the island from a serious attack, thus increasing their sway over the locals.

The low row of bricks pictured here along the shore at the Plaza San Carlos is all that remains of the old fort. (Author's collection.)

Luis Aury

Luis Aury was born in Paris. He was something of a privateer, and circumstances brought him to Venezuela where he worked with Simon Bolivar. From there, he moved to Galveston and worked to free Mexico from Spanish control. Aury did not always get along well with others. That led to his separation from Bolivar and, eventually, the Mexican revolutionaries. He was aware of MacGregor's dealings on Amelia Island, so when Galveston was no longer a welcome place for him, he set sail for Florida. He was not aware MacGregor had left Amelia when he arrived on September 21, 1817, just days after the battle at McClure's Hill.

Aury brought about 130 soldiers of Haitian descent with him, and more importantly, about $60,000. The island was in much need of that capital. Hubbard and Irwin pleaded with Aury, and after some tense arguing, Aury agreed to pay off most of the debts MacGregor had incurred in exchange for the title of commander-in-chief of military and naval forces of the Mexican Republic. Aury raised yet another flag over the island as a sovereign state. Hubbard and Irwin were given official titles as well. All of this had little to do with the nation we know as Mexico.

Aury's money settled the island's financial problems, but the men he brought caused a social uproar. They were mulattos and quarreled openly with the whites loyal to Hubbard. This caused significant strife that was difficult for the leaders to deal with. Hubbard fell ill in late October, and Aury used that as an opportunity to take further control of Amelia from him.

Hubbard died from yellow fever on October 26, prompting Aury to declare himself the supreme civil and military authority on the island. He welcomed smuggling and illegal trade into the United States, which was still working under the Non-Intercourse Act. For a short time, this was quite profitable. In order to make his government appear more legitimate, Aury held elections and created a legislature. Irwin was elected president, but the office held little power.

These actions did not please US president James Monroe. He evoked a special act that allowed the United States to use military force to defeat foreign powers attempting to occupy Spanish Florida. As Aury became aware of this and US warships appeared in the harbor, he knew defense was futile. He surrendered and the United States held Amelia Island in trust for Spain. This eventually led to negotiations with Spain that gave all of Florida to the United States by 1821.

Aury went on to New Granada, or what is now the nation of Columbia, and worked for independence there. He died about three and a half years later from injuries sustained after he was thrown from a horse. (Courtesy Florida State Archives.)

Duncan Lamont Clinch

It is worth noting that while Amelia Island saw its own trials and tribulations, the rest of Northeast Florida was embroiled in the Seminole Wars. History counts three of these, and the first was spurred by Gen. Andrew Jackson's attack on Seminole settlements that were both sympathetic to escaped slaves and that worked against the efforts of American settlers who tried to expand into Spanish Florida.

A result of the First Seminole War was to push the Seminoles onto a reservation in Central Florida. The Seminoles continued to assist escaped slaves, and from time to time would wander from their reservation. Thus, they were forced to move west of the Mississippi River, which eventually led to a second war.

Gen. Duncan Lamont Clinch served under Jackson and primarily oversaw the southern Georgia operations during the First Seminole War. After that, he led the army units in Florida tasked with keeping watch over the Native Americans on their reservations. He was active and served during the Second Seminole War but retired before its end and settled on a plantation near St. Marys, Georgia, across the Amelia River from Fernandina. He was elected to the US House of Representatives in 1844 but served just one term and did not seek reelection.

With his time in St. Marys, it is quite reasonable to believe Clinch visited Amelia Island. However, his actions here would not have been of any great consequence, and there is no real evidence he ever did visit. Still, his name remains essential to Amelia Island. Construction on Fort Clinch began in 1847 on the north end of Amelia Island. That was two years before the general's death, so perhaps that gave him time to come and accept the honor of seeing the fort that bears his name and still stands as part of one of the area's best-known state parks and military installations. (Courtesy Amelia Island Museum of History.)

CHAPTER TWO

The Rise of "New" Fernandina

Following the United States' acquisition of Florida in 1821, Amelia Island became part of a US territory. This territorial period was relatively quiet locally. The rest of Florida saw expanded growth and fought contentious wars with the Seminole Indians who the United States wished to remove from its new holding. These had little impact on Fernandina though. Sawmills that planed lumber from Florida's thick forests developed in other parts of Nassau County and the surrounding areas. Much of that shipped from Fernandina.

The area that is now known as Old Town sits on a bluff that is jammed into a peninsula of land that is bounded by the Amelia River on the west and Egans Creek to the north and east. A small marsh extends from the river and encroaches upon the south. Up until the 1850s, nearly all of Amelia's remarkable history took place in and around this small area save for the goings on near the Harrison Plantation.

Today's historic downtown of Fernandina Beach had been a plantation belonging to Domingo Fernandez. He had come to Florida in the 1780s during Spain's second rule of the island. He collected land grants throughout Northeast Florida, primarily on Amelia. He lived on what he called Yellow Bluff Plantation, which was located in present-day downtown Fernandina Beach. Domingo died in 1833 and was survived by his wife, Mary Mattair, and four of their seven children.

Mary sold land to the US government for the construction of the Amelia Island Lighthouse, which was physically relocated from Cumberland Island, and left the rest of her Amelia Island holdings to her children upon her death in 1846. It was then that the stage was set for an unprecedented transformation in the town of Fernandina, a locale that had already seen more political change than any other in the United States.

A one-acre parcel would remain in reserve for the Fernandez family in perpetuity at Domingo's Yellow Bluff Plantation. That is his burial ground and still lies in a fenced area in the lot between St. Michael's Catholic Church and its parochial school on North Fourth Street. Most of the rest of the Fernandez family's Amelia Island holdings would soon welcome a new generation of people to Fernandina who would bring wealth and prosperity along with exciting new opportunities.

David Yulee

No one had more of an impact on Fernandina's history than David Yulee. He was born David Levy to a Jewish family, and moved to Florida as a child. He studied law and, in time, served in the US House of Representatives as a delegate from the Florida Territory. After Florida was granted statehood, Yulee was elected as the first Jewish senator in the United States. His election was no doubt in recognition of his tireless efforts to gain statehood for Florida.

Yulee had big plans for Fernandina. He lost his second bid for a seat in the Senate, and immediately turned his attention to his second dream. He wanted to build a railroad across the Florida peninsula—from Fernandina on the east coast to Cedar Key on the west. This would create a faster connection from the Gulf of Mexico to the Atlantic Ocean than sailing around the peninsula. He spent the years of 1851 to 1855 planning his railroad. That included the quiet purchase of Domingo Fernandez's estate from his heirs.

Yulee regained a Senate seat in 1855, and tracks began to be laid that same year. Yulee was not satisfied with the topography of Old Town for his railroad terminus, but owned a large estate just to its south. Thus, he met with the people of Old Town, told them of the opportunity his railroad would bring, and convinced them to relocate from Old Town to a "new" Fernandina. This was, of course, the former Fernandez estate and land Yulee owned, which he happily sold back to the people of Amelia Island.

He platted the streets of downtown Fernandina Beach that are familiar today, named them, and set aside land for parks and churches. He also wanted Amelia Island to be a tourist destination and built hotels, like the Florida House. Tracks continued to be laid across the state, and new cities, like Gainesville, sprouted up along the way in order to reap the benefits the railroad would bring. The first train ran in March 1861, but the operation stalled by April when the Civil War began.

Yulee served in the Confederate Congress during the war. Afterwards, he was convicted of treason and spent nine months in the prison at Fort Pulaski. Following that, he returned to Fernandina and rebuilt his railroad, which proved profitable. The railroad expanded, but as Yulee neared the end of his life, he sold his interests and moved to Washington, DC, in 1880. He died in 1886 and is buried at Oak Hill Cemetery in Washington. His Fernandina home, which was once at the corner of North Third and Alachua Streets, has since been razed. (Courtesy Florida State Archives.)

Joseph Finnegan

Yulee's chief partner was Joseph Finnegan. Finnegan had a sawmill in Jacksonville and practiced law. He was instrumental in Yulee's purchase of the Fernandez estate and built his own expansive home of 40 rooms bordered by North Eleventh and Twelfth Streets and Broome and Calhoun Streets. During the war, Finnegan led the Confederate troops at Florida's most notable Civil War Battle at Olustee.

When he returned to Fernandina following the war, Finnegan was surprised to find his home had been converted by the Union to an orphanage for black children. He used his legal prowess to reclaim it, but that was only so he could resell it under his own terms. The home no longer stands.

After serving a brief term as a state senator, Finnegan moved to Savannah to become a cotton broker. He had married well, twice. As a result, he had significant land holdings, including an orange grove near Rutledge, Florida. After Savannah, he moved to Rutledge until the end of his life. Finnegan is buried in the Old City Cemetery in Jacksonville. (Above, courtesy Florida State Archives; right, author's collection.)

Robert Schuyler

As growth in "new" Fernandina expanded, Robert Schuyler emerged as the town's most prominent architect. He oversaw the construction of many of the buildings that are still considered some of the town's most prominent, including St. Peters Episcopal Church, the Tabby House, the Old Schoolhouse, and the Fairbanks House. (Opposite bottom, author's collection; all others, courtesy Amelia Island Museum of History.)

High School. FERNANDINA, Fla.

John Mann

John Mann was the best-known local contractor during the era following the railroad's construction. He owned companies that supplied groceries and marine hardware and built many of the town's most notable historic buildings, such as Villa las Palmas, the Hoyt House, the John Denham Palmer house, several homes on North Sixth Street, the Keystone Hotel, and Memorial United Methodist Church. (Opposite bottom, author's collection; all others, courtesy Amelia Island Museum of History.)

Villa Las Palmas, Residence of Mayor Borden, Fernandina, Fla.

The Keystone—Fernandina's New Tourist Hotel.

Marcellus Williams

Marcellus Williams began his career surveying Spanish Land grants in Florida. Eventually, he came to be the surveyor for Yulee's railroad. He also partnered with Samuel Swann in his land dealings. The Williams house still stands at 103 South Ninth Street. Jefferson Davis, the president of the Confederacy, was a friend of Williams and stored some of his belongings in the home at one point during the war. (Courtesy Amelia Island Museum of History.)

Major Duryee

Maj. William Duryee first came to Amelia Island with Union forces who occupied it during the war. He returned afterward and placed his hand in several businesses, like a dry goods store and bank. The bank operated out of the building at the foot of Centre and Front Streets that is now the Marina Restaurant. Duryee was also the contractor for the Cumberland Island Jetty, and a pillar of St. Peters Episcopal Church. (Courtesy Amelia Island Museum of History.)

Samuel Swann

Like Duryee, Samuel Swann was an essential member of the St. Peters congregation and had considerable influence over many local commercial concerns. Swann had come to Fernandina to work with Joseph Finnegan as his bookkeeper. He also helped broker Finnegan's land deals, produced bricks, and even did a little blockade running for the Confederacy during the war.

Though he was a North Carolina native, Swann's knowledge of Florida real estate might have been unequaled. Along with Yulee and Finnegan, he completed a triumvirate brain trust that made the Florida Railroad possible. Swann's role was to leverage his real estate knowledge to snatch up Florida lands on which the tracks would be laid.

Community was essential to Swann. When he built his office building that still stands at the northwest corner of Centre and North Fourth Streets, he provided space for a library, ballroom, and gymnasium. The town's fire engine and the bell used to alert citizens of fires were housed in the back of the building.

Swann built two homes on Centre Street. Neither remains. The second was nicknamed the Cottage Ornee and was quite fine. It was located at the southwest corner of South Sixth and Centre Streets and is pictured here along with Swann. (Both, courtesy Amelia Island Museum of History.)

William Lohman

Of course, there were those involved in local politics. William Lohman operated the dry goods store seen in this picture at 10 North Second Street. He also constructed the building at South Sixth and Ash Streets, currently a hardware store. Lohman served as chairman of the Nassau County Commissioners. (Courtesy Amelia Island Museum of History.)

Maj. Fernando Suhrer

Lohman's father-in-law was the tax collector Maj. Fernando Suhrer, a German-born Union veteran of the war. Suhrer also ran a hotel called the Mansion House, which was destroyed by the 1887 fire. He was murdered on the steps of the Mansion House by the great-great-grandson of Thomas Jefferson, who had accused Suhrer of making disparaging comments about his wife. This was perhaps the most notorious local crime of the era. (Courtesy Amelia Island Museum of History.)

Samuel Riddell

Samuel Riddell was the local postmaster and served as mayor during the 1870s. His home, seen here, was once on North Fifth Street between Alachua and Broome Streets. In 1866, the steamer *Evening Star* sank off the coast of Georgia and made national headlines. Some of the survivors arrived in Fernandina on their lifeboats. Riddell took in one of those who was badly injured and nursed him back to health. (Courtesy Amelia Island Museum of History.)

William Naylor Thompson

William Naylor Thompson represented Fernandina in the state senate during its golden age at the end of the 19th century. He served on the Confederate side during the Civil War and first came to Fernandina to work with the railroad. His house at 11 South Seventh Street still stands. (Author's collection.)

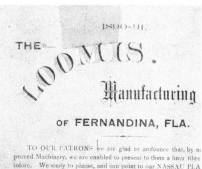

Silas and Edwin Loomis

Silas Loomis and his son Edwin are seldom spoken of in Fernandina's history, but they were harbingers of things to come to the island. Silas was an accomplished scientist who established a factory with his son that made a fiber from palms and palmetto. That fiber was used as components of cable insulation, plaster and stucco, mattresses, and paper. Of course, the current paper mills on the island now make multipurpose fibers. The Loomis plant was destroyed by the 1898 hurricane. That and a new rival product from Africa ultimately doomed the company. The tattered remains of an advertisement for the company are seen here. (Courtesy Amelia Island Museum of History.)

Hinton James Baker

Hinton James Baker came to Fernandina to work as the attorney for the Florida Railroad. He served as county judge and authored the city's charter. His father, Archibald Baker, was the first minister of the local Presbyterian church. Reverend Baker's home, seen here, still stands a block away from the church at 112 North Sixth Street. Judge Baker's son Hinton J. Baker Jr. was also a prominent local attorney. (Author's collection.)

George Fairbanks

Among Fernandina's most accomplished citizens was George R. Fairbanks. He served as a state senator shortly after Florida gained statehood and served as president of the Florida Fruit Growers Association. Though born in New York, he aligned with the Confederacy during the war and rose to the rank of major in the Army of Tennessee. He was a founder of the University of the South in Sewanee.

In 1879, Fairbanks was recruited to Fernandina by David Yulee to serve as editor for the local newspaper, the *Florida Mirror*. Fairbanks developed a passion for Florida history and taught himself Spanish to decipher the Spanish records concerning the peninsula. He published several books on the state's history.

His impressive home still stands at 227 South Seventh Street. The home is often referred to as Fairbanks's Folly. It is said he built the home and furnished it as a surprise gift to his wife. However, the gift was not received as well as planned. From the home's tower, Fairbanks and his granddaughter could see Jacksonville's devastating fire in 1901. (Courtesy Amelia Island Museum of History.)

Louis Hirth

Louis Hirth no doubt learned his trade in Germany before immigrating to Fernandina. He established a bar on North Third Street in 1898. Five years later, he opened the Palace Saloon at the corner of North Second and Centre Streets. That remains Florida's oldest bar. Hirth converted it to an ice cream parlor during Prohibition. (Courtesy Amelia Island Museum of History.)

Nathaniel B. Borden

Nathaniel B. Borden is seen here on the right beside a large Florida poplar log that was shipped to Germany in 1921. Borden dealt in lumber. He served briefly as mayor and was among the town's more colorful characters. He is perhaps best known for building the expansive Villa las Palmas mansion on Alachua Street in 1910 (see page 28). He did so as a gift for his 17-year-old fiancée, Flossie. The fact that he was several decades older than her must have been scandalous at the time. Indeed, a local legend tells that Borden took Flossie's father out on his boat to ask for her hand in marriage. When her father refused, Borden threw him overboard. (Courtesy Amelia Island Museum of History.)

Fred Hoyt
Borden's home was constructed by John Mann, who also built the Hoyt House at the corner of South Eighth Street and Atlantic Avenue (see page 29). That home belonged to Fred W. Hoyt. Hoyt is responsible for the large building across North Second Street from the Palace Saloon where he sold groceries, furniture, and shipping supplies. He also established a local bank in 1887. He is seen in the center of the back row in this picture of an early local baseball club. (Courtesy Amelia Island Museum of History.)

James and William Bell
Captains James and William Bell were identical twins. Both men worked as river pilots, helping to guide ships into the Fernandina harbor. They built a couple of homes on the island including the gingerbread-laden structure at the northeast corner of Beech and South Eighth Streets that belonged to William. James's impressive home is seen here. It presides over the Plaza San Carlos at Old Town and was featured in the 1988 film *The Adventures of Pippi Longstocking*. (Author's collection.)

Emma Love Hardee

Of course, women played important roles in Fernandina's development. Emma Love Hardee was very active in civic affairs. A leader in the First Presbyterian Church, she worked especially hard for poor and sick children through the Ladies Civic League and Woman's Club. Hardee also helped to serve disadvantaged children through the schools by organizing things like a school lunch program. Emma Love Hardee Elementary School on Susan Drive is named in her honor. She is pictured here with her family around 1915. (Courtesy Sapp family collection.)

Flossie Borden

Flossie Borden was the 17-year-old bride of the aforementioned Nathaniel Borden. Flossie was known for her spirited personality. She is seen here driving an early automobile that belonged to her. It was one of the town's first, and it is said she was involved in the town's first wreck. (Courtesy Amelia Island Museum of History.)

Kate Bailey

Kate Bailey was married to Effingham Bailey. They made their home at the corner of Ash and South Seventh Streets in one of the best-known homes on the island. The Queen Anne Victorian structure was completed in 1895.

Kate grew up in a home on the adjacent lot. Her own lot was a gift from her father, who managed the local Florida Railroad operations. Her grandfather spent his career working at Harrison Plantation on the south end of the island.

Kate was known for her musical talents, particularly on the piano. She often played from a front room of the home, and passersby would often stop to enjoy a moment of her free concerts. She composed the Fernandina Beach High School alma mater, which is still used.

There is a tree that forks Ash Street very close to the Bailey House. It is said that when it came time to pave Fernandina's roads, Kate sat on her porch with a shotgun as a silent threat to any worker who dared cut down her tree. Indeed, the tree is still referred to as "Kate's Oak." Bailey is seen above seated in the window of the Tabby House across South Seventh Street from her own home, which is seen below as it stands today. (Above, courtesy Amelia Island Museum of History; below, author's collection.)

Jane Fernandez Villalongo

Jane Fernandez Villalongo was the daughter of Domingo Fernandez and Mary Mattair, who owned the estate that is now downtown Fernandina. Jane and her sister Elizabeth were in possession of the estate after inheriting it when the deal to sell it was brokered. It was Jane who insisted one acre be preserved for her family in perpetuity. (Courtesy Amelia Island Museum of History.)

Lucy Coleman Carnegie

Lucy Carnegie was never technically a resident of Fernandina or Amelia Island, but she must have been a presence. She was the wife of Thomas Carnegie, who built a famed steel empire with his brother Andrew, making them the wealthiest men in the world. Thomas and Lucy purchased nearly all of Cumberland Island in 1881. Thomas died before the Carnegies' expansive mansion was completed there, but Lucy and her children lived in the home. With very little community to speak of on Cumberland, Fernandina often provided a sense of society to her and her family. Lucy's daughter converted the Greyfield house on Cumberland to an inn in 1962 and was a strong advocate for Cumberland's preservation. (Courtesy Amelia Island Museum of History.)

Chloe Merrick Reed

Chloe Merrick Reed came to Fernandina in 1863 and acquired the home that still stands at 102 South Tenth Street through a tax sale of abandoned Confederate properties. Next, she set to work educating the children of freed slaves. Working with the Freedman's Bureau, she founded a school and orphanage.

In August 1869, she married Harrison Reed, who, at the time, was the governor of Florida. He served until 1873, which gave Chloe plenty of time to exert her influence as first lady of the state. She fought for legislation that aided the poor and improved education. She is included in the state's list of Great Floridians. (Courtesy Florida State Archives.)

Mary Martha Reid

Another "Reed," phonetically at least, with ties to a former Florida governor is Mary Martha Reid. She was born in St. Marys, Georgia, in 1812 but spent most of her childhood on a plantation on Amelia Island. In 1836, she married Robert R. Reid, who was the judge of the US Superior Court for East Florida based in St. Augustine. In that capacity, he tutored a young Florida attorney, David Levy Yulee. In 1839, Robert was appointed governor of the Florida Territory by Martin Van Buren.

Mary Martha and Robert had two sons before he died of yellow fever in 1841. Mary Martha then began teaching school in Fernandina and Jacksonville to provide income for her and her children, though one son tragically died within a year of his father's death. At the outbreak of the Civil War, her surviving son who she called "Jenks" enlisted in the Confederate army and was stationed in Virginia. In short time, Mary Martha moved to Richmond to be closer to him.

Each of the Confederate states was expected to establish a hospital in Richmond to serve its own natives. Mary Martha felt a calling and took this task to heart. She and Dr. Thomas Palmer converted a Richmond mansion into a 150-bed hospital. Palmer oversaw the medical care, and Reid performed nursing duties. She also spent countless hours soliciting donations for the hospital and writing thank-you letters to contributors. Many of her appeals and letters were published in Florida newspapers, and Reid's notoriety quickly grew. In time, she was known as the "Mother of Florida boys." The hospital served 1,000 young men in its first year.

After the war, she returned to teaching in Florida, this time in Palatka. As her years waned, she moved to Fernandina to live with her niece. Mary Martha Reid died in Fernandina in 1896 and is buried at St. Peters Episcopal Cemetery. This stained-glass window at St. Peters Episcopal Church hangs in her memory.

One interesting Fernandina footnote to Mary Martha Reid is that her sister Rebecca Smith was the second wife of Joseph Finnegan. Smith's daughter, Martha, from her first marriage married Samuel Swann and was the same niece with whom Mary Martha Reid lived out her last years. (Author's collection.)

IN MEMORIAM
MARY MARTHA REID
BORN 1812 ✦ DIED 1884

The Sisters of St. Joseph

These are the Sisters of St. Joseph. In the second row, second from right, is Sister Josephine, who was the last remaining of the original group that came from La Puy, France. The rest of the group's predecessors are more noteworthy. They originally came to Fernandina to teach freed slave children. In 1887, a terrible yellow fever epidemic struck the town, infecting as much as 70 percent of the population. Most of those who were not affected left town. The Sisters of St. Joseph chose to stay. Four brave women worked tirelessly to aid the infirm, regardless of race or creed. The brave act cost two of them their lives. The graves of the French contingent are seen below at Bosque Bello Cemetery. (Above, courtesy Amelia Island Museum of History; below, author's collection.)

Emma Delaney

Amelia Island is also rich with African American history. There were several well-established churches attended by the black population during Fernandina's golden age, and their congregations were integral parts of the town. Among the standouts in the local community, indeed the world community, was Emma Delaney.

She was born in Fernandina in 1871. She spent her childhood learning at the local catholic convent and then moved on to Spellman College, where she studied to be a Baptist missionary. Supported in part by the congregation at First Missionary Baptist Church on South Ninth Street, she left for Africa in 1899 as a missionary. She was the first female African American to do that.

Delaney stayed in Africa until 1906 in the area that is now Malawi and established schools and churches. She then returned to the United States and began speaking about her experiences. Her focus during this time was to raise awareness and funds for a return trip to Africa, which she made in 1912. This trip took her to East Africa in the area that is now Liberia.

This time, she stayed in Africa until the early 1920s, when she finally returned to the United States. She died in Fernandina in 1922, and her grave at Bosque Bello Cemetery is seen here. She is included on the list of the state's Great Floridians. (Courtesy Florida State Archives.)

William H. Peck

William H. Peck (second row, third from left) came to Fernandina in the mid-1880s from Virginia to work at the new high school for African Americans in Nassau County. The head of the school died in the 1887 yellow fever epidemic, and Peck was named as his replacement. He held that title for the next 50 years. He worked tirelessly to improve the curriculum at the school, and when a new school was built in 1928, it was named in his honor. From that point forward, Peck worked at the same school that bore his name. Peck High School was closed when segregation ended. The building is a now a community center. (Courtesy Amelia Island Museum of History.)

Liberty Billings

Liberty Billings first came to Fernandina in 1865 after serving as a lieutenant colonel in the first-ever African American US Army unit during the Civil War. Upon his arrival in Fernandina, he quickly became a leader in black rights in Florida. He conducted the 1870 census in Nassau County and served as state senator for Nassau, Duval, and Clay Counties during most of the 1870s. He too is listed as a Great Floridian. This home at 222 North Fifth Street once belonged to his family, and his Great Floridian plaque hangs here. (Author's collection.)

Abraham Lincoln Lewis

Abraham Lincoln Lewis was born in Madison County in 1865 to parents of former slaves. His father was a blacksmith by trade and named his son after the president who had freed him. Abraham preferred his initials though, and most commonly referred to himself as A.L.

Lewis's family moved to Jacksonville, and A.L. spent a little time in public school but had to leave in order to get a job to help the family. He worked at a lumber mill, and in time was promoted to foreman, making him the highest paid black individual there. Lewis always sought to escape the rut of poverty and so was a diligent saver. He worked at the lumber mill for 20 years and was able to use a portion of his savings to invest in a shoe store. He also married the great-granddaughter of Zephaniah Kingsley, the successful owner of Kingsley Plantation on Fort George Island.

By 1901, Lewis and a group of six other African Americans recognized the need for an insurance corporation to serve other blacks. Investing $100 each, they formed what would eventually become the Afro-American Life Insurance Company. Within a year, the company was making a profit of $50 a week. Lewis certainly met his goal of escaping poverty and became the first black millionaire in Florida.

In the 1920s and 1930s, the company began sponsoring outings for employees to Franklintown, a small black settlement at the south end of Amelia Island. These became quite popular with employees, but Lewis noted that recreational outings and opportunities for blacks were hampered by Jim Crow laws. So, in 1935, he bought 33 acres along the beach near Franklintown with the idea of establishing a vacation destination for other African Americans. He called the project American Beach.

Lewis platted streets, naming them after the insurance company's founders, and sold lots so others could build vacation homes. He bought adjacent tracts of land to expand the endeavor. Not everyone could afford to purchase property, but that did not stop throngs of sun-seekers from visiting. Hotels, restaurants, and nightclubs that hosted famous performers and served the tourists also came along. American Beach thrived during the 1930s and through the 1960s. The end of desegregation saw the destination's popularity wane, but it remains a mostly African American community with a strong sense of history.

A.L. Lewis died in 1947. He is buried at Memorial Cemetery in Jacksonville. (Courtesy Amelia Island Museum of History.)

CHAPTER THREE

Building Today's Amelia Island

As all good things do, Amelia Island's golden age came to an end. That process began in the late 1800s, when Henry Flagler began construction on his Florida East Coast Railway, which bypassed Fernandina and focused on St. Augustine instead.

Flagler was a product of New York and became John Rockefeller's partner in the Standard Oil Corporation. He might not have been quite as famous as his partner, but even Rockefeller admitted that Flagler was the true brains behind the operation. Their partnership made Flagler extraordinarily wealthy.

Flagler first began visiting Florida in 1878 on the advice of his doctor concerning his wife, who had taken ill. She died within two years, but Flagler remarried and continued to visit the Sunshine State. He recognized that there was tremendous potential in Florida as a tourist destination, but little of that existed along the East Coast beyond St. Augustine. His Florida visits left him enamored with the Ancient City, and so he based his operations there. He built the Ponce de Leon Hotel, which opened in St. Augustine in 1888, and eventually extended his railroad all the way down to Key West, with stops at other hotels he owned along the way.

Flagler's railroad sparked the development of much of present-day Florida, but it created hardships on Amelia Island. It redirected many of the tourists who would have visited Fernandina. The process of dredging Tampa Bay began in the early 20th century, and the infrastructure of Fernandina's docks began to fail. These factors combined to see many of the shipping operations leave Amelia.

This meant Fernandina and Amelia Island needed to find new economic opportunities. They did so in the late 1930s, when the Container Corporation and Rayonier built pulp mills on the island. This created a blue-collar atmosphere that would pervade until the construction of resorts at the south end of the island beginning in the 1970s. The paper mill and tourist industries are mostly responsible, directly or indirectly, for bringing the people who made today's local community. Their stories are explored in this chapter.

O.H. Anderson

With the local shipping industry falling off and the city on an economic slide, city leaders put out a $25,000 reward for anyone who could attract a pulp and paper mill to the area. The call was answered by city manager O.H. Anderson. In fact, two mills would come to Fernandina, but the city was disinterested in fulfilling their financial promise. Anderson sued the city, and the case went to the state supreme court, which decided in his favor. The impact of Anderson's efforts to attract the mills, however arduous they may have been, cannot be understated. The mills provided a new backbone to a town that had lost its previous one. This is a photograph of the Rayonier Mill's foundation being poured. (Courtesy Amelia Island Museum of History.)

Jack Woodward

The coming of the mills brought new jobs, which meant more people would come to town. These people needed places to live, and it was time for Fernandina to expand away from downtown. Jack Woodward owned a car dealership and was a partner in the Forest Hills subdivision that developed the area around Stanley Drive and Egans Creek. Taken as the area was being developed, this photograph looks east on Highland Street from North Eighteenth Street in the mid-1940s. (Courtesy City of Fernandina Beach.)

Hymie Fishler

Woodward's partner in his developments was Hymie Fishler. Fishler was an attorney who served the Ocean Highway and Port Authority, City of Fernandina Beach, and Nassau County School Board during the mid-20th century. Those roles gave him considerable local influence during this time. Woodward played a vital role in the partnership since he could effectively execute much of the processes needed for the developments that could have become conflicts of interests for Fishler acting alone.

At one point, Fishler considered a plan that would have connected Amelia with some of the small islands in the Amelia River, like Tiger Island. There was even talk of building a bridge to St. Marys, Georgia. The only part of this plan that was ever really completed was the construction of the North Fourteenth Street Bridge over Egans Creek.

These are photographs of Fishler with his wife, Esther, as well as a small display honoring Fishler that sits at the Nassau Center at Florida State College at Jacksonville. (Above, courtesy Amelia Island Museum of History; right, author's collection.)

William Corkum
Shrimping was another essential part of the local economy in the early 20th century in Fernandina. That was due in large part to a confluence of shrimping innovators in Fernandina. William Corkum adapted the otter trawl. This allowed shrimpers to drag the ocean's bottom for shrimp, where they are found in great concentration. (Courtesy Amelia Island Museum of History.)

William Jones Davis
Capt. William Jones Davis was another innovator in the shrimping industry. He was the first to use a power-driven boat to drag a net. In addition to shrimping, Davis worked as a local harbor pilot. Capt. George T. Davis, his son, was also a local harbor pilot for many years. William Jones Davis is seen here fifth from left. (Courtesy Amelia Island Museum of History.)

David Cook

David Cook made some innovative modifications to Corkum's otter trawl design by adding corners and wings. At one point, Cook operated a fleet of 10 shrimp boats that were based in Fernandina. Early sketches of otter trawls are seen here. (Courtesy Amelia Island Museum of History.)

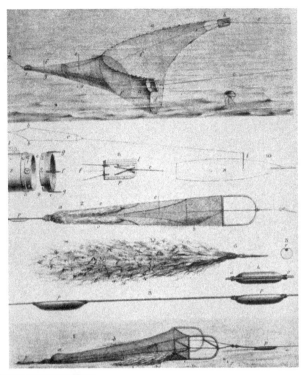

Harry Sahlman

Harry Sahlman was a reluctant shrimper. He was a lumber salesman who took possession of a shrimp boat from its builder who could not find a buyer. Sahlman took the boat to recover his debts and ended up building a shrimping empire that is still in operation, though it now does much of its work in Central America. Sahlman bought Villa las Palmas from Nathaniel Borden and is pictured here with his wife, Melba. (Courtesy Amelia Island Museum of History.)

Mike Tiliakos and Jimmy Deonas

Shrimping brought others to the area. Mike Tiliakos came to Fernandina from Greece in 1912 in order to begin building shrimp boats. In the early 1940s, another young man from Greece joined him. This was Dematrios "Jimmy" Deonas. Deonas quickly became a leader at the boatyard and married Tiliakos's daughter, Anna. Deonas had significant skill in boat design. His design for boats with larger engines that could reach deeper waters with larger nets was an innovation for the entire industry. Boat orders poured in.

Upon Jimmy's death, his son Nick took over operations at the boatyard, which was located where Beech Street once dead ended at the waterfront. Nick and his son Jimmy are both active and influential in local politics. Tiliakos is seen above. On the opposite page, Jimmy Deonas poses in the windows of a shrimp boat under construction. Jimmy's son Nick is seen with Curtis "Topsy" Smith on page 81, and as a boy on page 63. (Courtesy Deonas family collection.)

William Burbank

Around 1915, William Burbank began making the nets used to shrimp. He did his own shrimping in addition to net making, but the latter quickly proved to be more profitable. His sons carried on the family business, and the company still makes nets, though they have repositioned into the sports industry. This photograph features, from left to right, Billy Jr., William Sr., Frank Burbank, and Billy III. (Courtesy Amelia Island Museum of History.)

Exteen Corbett

Exteen Corbett served in the Army during World War I. He was born in Two Egg, Florida, a small town just west of the Apalachicola River in the panhandle, and came to Fernandina in 1930 to stay with family. His brother Tracy was working for a local factory that processed menhaden, or pogy. These fish were caught offshore, then the factory converted them into an oil that was used for other agricultural functions. Tracy eventually took ownership of the "pogy plant," and Exteen himself took over operation in 1949.

Corbett's local influence reached far beyond the plant, however. He served two terms as city commissioner and was an important member of Memorial United Methodist Church. He was a founding member of the local Kiwanis Club and served as president for that group. Corbett's other business ventures included Florida National Bank, where he served on the board of directors. He passed away in 2004. Above is an aerial view of the pogy plant, and Exteen Corbett is at left. (Above, courtesy Amelia Island Museum of History; left, courtesy Corbett family collection.)

Paul Burns

Paul Burns served on the city commission with Exteen Corbett. He sold insurance and was one of the leaders in local real estate through the last half of the 1900s. He was a founding member of the Amelia Island Board of Realtors and the chamber of commerce. Burns was a local philanthropist and made many contributions over the years to organizations like Baranbas Center, Habitat for Humanity, and Meals on Wheels. He was also a key member of St. Peters Episcopal Church. (Courtesy Purvis family collection.)

Bill Melton and Ben Sorensen

The 1950s and 1960s were relatively free from controversy in Fernandina. There were a handful of local leaders who cycled through the city commission and made impactful decisions that few seriously questioned. People like the aforementioned Burns, Corbett, and Fishler were among this group, as were Bill Melton and Ben Sorensen. Sorensen is seen here on the right while serving as mayor at the dedication of the Marine Welcome Station in 1964. Sorensen worked for Rayonier and was a long-tenured city commissioner both in Fernandina and Fernandina Beach, which were two separate municipalities. Melton had holdings at the beach and also served as mayor. He is seen at center right in the photograph on the bottom of the following page in the flowered shirt. (Courtesy City of Fernandina Beach.)

Eldridge Partin

Eldridge Partin took over the operations of Partin's Shoes and Menswear Store at 313 Centre Street in 1959. His father had started the store. Partin was a Rotarian and leader in Memorial United Methodist Church. He played a role in the redesigning of Centre Street in 1978. His sister Annie was married to Paul Burns. (Courtesy Blalock family collection.)

H.J. Youngblood

H.J. Youngblood started out as head of the roads department for Nassau County. That meant one of his duties was overseeing chain gangs charged with construction of some of the growing county's roadways. That position suited him, so he eventually chose to run for sheriff. He spent the next 28 years in that capacity, more than any other person in Nassau County. Youngblood was legendary and peacefully guided Amelia Island through difficult times, such as desegregation. His grandson is NFL Hall of Famer Jack Youngblood. H.J. Youngblood is seen in the bottom right corner of this photograph, in the glasses, at a meeting of the Kiwanis Club at the Seaside Inn in the 1950s. (Courtesy City of Fernandina Beach Archives.)

Sandy McArthur

Alexander G. McArthur, better known as Sandy, moved to Nassau County in 1927. In 1934, he was elected to the Florida Senate and served until 1954. McArthur lived on a large estate near Amelia City and is credited with bringing peacocks to the area. There is still a population of peacocks that roam the Summer Beach neighborhoods near the Ritz Carlton, though their presence is controversial. McArthur also worked for Rayonier as a timber manager and operated N.G. Wade Investment Co. of Jacksonville. (Courtesy Florida State Archives.)

Ray Caldwell

The *News-Leader* is the primary source for local news and is Florida's oldest weekly newspaper. Ray Caldwell took over publishing duties there in 1959. Caldwell was well known and respected throughout town for running a paper with fair reporting at a time before the internet when newspapers reigned supreme. Caldwell was influential behind the scenes as many local leaders turned to him for his always sound advice. His grave at Bosque Bello Cemetery is seen here. (Courtesy Amelia Island Museum of History.)

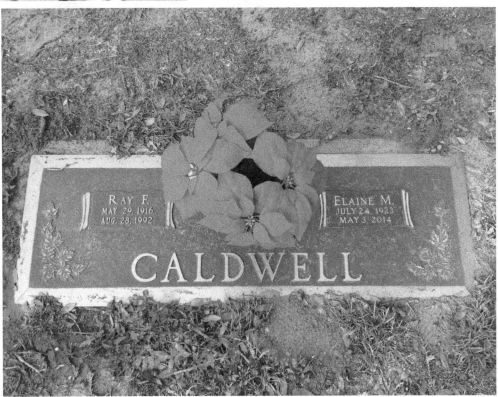

Ed and Stella Moore

David Yulee's Strathmore hotel at the beach was destroyed by the 1898 hurricane. It was replaced by a publicly owned casino that included a restaurant, bathrooms, showers, a bowling alley, and skating rink. That was the only structure of significance at the beach until Moore's opened in 1929 by Morris and Claire Moore. It included a small restaurant and grocery store as well as a couple of rental units.

That burned in 1932, but was quickly rebuilt with expanded facilities. Eventually, their son Ed and his wife, Stella, took over the operations. Moore's became the center of beach activity on Amelia Island as the beach became increasingly popular and the island's population rose with the addition of the mills. As a result, Ed Moore continued to expand the scope of his business, but a 1964 fire spelled its demise. Pictured are Ed and Stella behind the counter, and the exterior of the original 1929 Moore's building. (Both, courtesy Moore family collection.)

Picnic Grounds, Gerbings Gardens, Fernandina Beach, Fla.

Gus Gerbing

Gus Gerbing lived near Amelia City. In 1923, as a young man, he started growing camellias to sell. Gerbing did well with the flowers and opened Gerbing Gardens to the public on the banks of the Amelia River in 1932. The garden, seen here, was a success and was widely regarded as among the best public gardens in the region. Gerbing had a deep passion for camellias and was considered a world expert on them. One species bears his name. (Courtesy Amelia Island Museum of History.)

Thomas J. Shave

There are two bridges that connect Amelia Island to the mainland. The more traveled of those is the Thomas J. Shave Jr. Bridge, which connects Fernandina with Yulee via A1A. It was completed in 1978. Shave was a local attorney and judge. The other bridge, at the south end of the island, was named for state representative George Crady. Along with other county officials, Shave is pictured here seated at far left while he served as county attorney. (Courtesy City of Fernandina Beach.)

Mary Agnes Wolff White

Mary Agnes White was a beloved local resident who had a hand in starting the Amelia Island Museum of History, the Magnolia Garden Club, and other ventures on the island. She and her husband, Bob, bought a fifth share of Fernandina Lumber and Supply Company, which they owned with Sandy McArthur and Ernest and Stuart Davis. Eventually, the Whites held the company in whole during a time when there was much construction happening locally. Mary Agnes's father, Dr. George Ralph Wolff, was a popular local dentist. His name is found on a local street and a park at Main Beach. (Courtesy White family collection.)

William Decker

William Decker worked as a caretaker at Fort Clinch. He was an avid local historian and had a sizeable collection of Amelia Island artifacts. Decker even lived in a historic Old Town home, the "Pippi House." He also had an extensive butterfly collection that was exhibited at the 1933 World's Fair. Upon his death, William Decker's son Doug sold the collection of local artifacts to the city; the city then donated it to the Duncan Lamont Clinch Historical Society. This was the seed from which the Amelia Island Museum of History would grow. (Courtesy Amelia Island Museum of History.)

Sarah Alice Broadbent

Sarah Alice Broadbent is likely the most mysterious person in the history of Amelia Island. She was a recluse who lived on Crane Island, a small piece of land near the airport and barely separated from Amelia by a marshy area. She was born sometime around the 1880s and lived with her father, who was English. He died in 1921, but Sarah Alice continued to live reclusively on the island.

She purposely distanced herself from others on Amelia Island, but did come over from time to time for business or to obtain things she could not provide on her own. She wore a dress made from old flour sacks and fastened with buttons she probably picked up somewhere. She did not wear shoes, so when she came into Fernandina to conduct business, she would cross the muddy marsh barefooted, traipse through the brush, and walk along the railroad until she got to wherever she was going.

Her poor attire must have been a sight for the locals, and her actions contributed to the spectacle. She never came to town without her shotgun in tow, and she engaged others as little as possible. She came to deal with matters related to her property and perhaps to trade or purchase a few things, but she did not socialize.

There were a few people whom she trusted, however, and with whom she had at least a superficial working relationship. For example, there were a few farmers with land near Crane Island on Amelia. She would, on occasion, help work in their fields. Broadbent had a disdain for anyone who tried to come over to her island, however. She was once arrested for using her shotgun to threaten a group of engineers charged with surveying the flow of water around the island. A proud woman, she refused to eat while in jail because accepting the food given to her meant accepting charity. When she eventually relented, she did so only with the understanding the debt would eventually be repaid. Thus, she sent vegetables she had grown to the jail until the debt was repaid many times over.

In addition to the engineers, many who came too close to the island by boat could attest to her distrust for visitors. Those passing close to the island might expect her to pop out of the woods with her shotgun pointed in their direction. Once, a gentleman was found floating in a boat near Crane Island, dead from a gunshot. There was nothing to link anyone to any crime and nothing was ever made of the incident, but it was widely suspected that Broadbent was the culprit.

One November evening in 1952, Sheriff H.J. Youngblood noticed a glow in the sky over the west side of Amelia island. He went out to Crane Island the next morning and found the ruins of Broadbent's home still smoldering. Charred bones were found, but there were discarded bones everywhere and it was never determined whether those inside the house were animal or human. Whatever the case, Broadbent was never seen or heard from again, though no death certificate was ever issued.

This picture was taken the day after the home burned. Nick Deonas is the child in the picture. (Courtesy Amelia Island Museum of History.)

Thomas Patrick O'Hagan

Thomas Patrick O'Hagan served as keeper of the Amelia Island Lighthouse from 1905 to 1925. At that point, his son Thomas John O'Hagan took over the duties. The O'Hagans lived in a small house beside the lighthouse. The whole family is pictured here on the steps of that home. The lighthouse was moved to Amelia from Cumberland Island in 1838 and is the oldest lighthouse in Florida. (Courtesy Amelia Island Museum of History.)

Hal Belcher

Like so many others, Hal Belcher first came to Fernandina to work for a paper mill. Rayonier hired him in 1948. Belcher had a keen interest in the history of Amelia Island. His areas of expertise included the lighthouse, which he helped maintain, and Bosque Bello Cemetery, about which he published books. Belcher passed away in 2013. (Courtesy Belcher family collection.)

Willie Mae Ashley

Willie Mae Ashley also made significant contributions to what is known about local history. She was born in Fernandina in 1922 and spent her childhood here. She graduated from Peck High School in 1940 before attending Bethune-Cookman University, where she earned her bachelor's degree. She attended the University of Michigan and Florida A&M University to earn her master's degree.

Ashley married and returned to Nassau County to teach. She started in a one-room school in Chester, but eventually made her way back to Peck. She was an involved teacher and served as president of the Nassau County Teachers Association. After her retirement, she helped lead efforts to restore and preserve Peck High School. The auditorium is now named in her honor.

She held a keen interest in her own African roots and in those of others. She traveled to Africa and wrote "The Ebony Connection," a manuscript that traces the ancestry of many in the local African American community. Ashley researched the local African missionary Emma Delaney. Her exploration into Delaney's life was inexhaustible and culminated in the 1987 book *Far from Home*. Ashley passed away in October 2014. (Courtesy Amelia Island Museum of History.)

Helen Gordon Litrico

Helen Gordon Litrico moved to Fernandina in 1970 with her husband, Gino, a local native. Helen was an early employee of Amelia Island Plantation and worked as director of public relations. In 1975, she founded *Amelia Now*, a local quarterly magazine that is still in publication and operated by her son Charles. Through *Amelia Now* and work with other groups supporting local history, she has made valuable contributions to local historical research and preservation efforts. (Courtesy Litrico family collection.)

Dee Dee Bartels

Dee Dee Bartels is a Key West native who moved to Fernandina in the mid-1950s. She moved away for a time but ended up coming back. Bartels owned local shrimp boats and played a role in creating the events that would evolve into the annual Shrimp Festival. Bartels is another supporter of local historic preservation efforts. The public boat ramp at the end of North Fourteenth Street is named in her honor. (Author's collection.)

Melvin Dougherty

Melvin Dougherty grew up in Fernandina Beach and his career was highlighted by the role of Nassau County building inspector. He was a veteran who served in the Marines during World War II and was very active in the local American Legion Post No. 54. The war memorial at the foot of Centre Street is largely his doing. He assisted in the National Historic District registration as well.

Dougherty was also a shrimper and was one of the founding fathers of the annual Shrimp Festival. He and a group of shrimpers started the event in 1963 as a shrimp boat racing competition. Dougherty chaired the committee for 14 years. The Shrimp Festival is now renowned and brings over 100,000 people annually to the event that is always held the first weekend in May. (Courtesy Johnson family collection.)

Fernandina Pirates Club

The Fernandina Pirates Club is iconic. The club started in 1973. Initially only men could join, but women were admitted beginning in the 1980s. Members must learn "pirate skills" like loading and firing black powder weapons and understand the club's strict safety procedures. The group's mission is not actually very pirate-like. They exist to serve and represent the community at various events. Dressed in full pirate garb, they attend all types of local gatherings and give away beads or other pirate paraphernalia to children along with a hearty "Arrrrgh." This photograph is from one of the early Shrimp Festival's Invasion of the Pirates, an annual marquee event for the group. (Courtesy Amelia Island Museum of History.)

Suzanne Davis Hardee

There are some dynastic families in Fernandina. Suzanne Davis Hardee (opposite) was at the heart of one of those. She was born to Ernest Percival (E.P.) Davis Sr. and Edna Mizell in Crandall, Florida, in 1922. The Mizell name itself is legendary in parts of Florida, especially around Orlando. In Nassau County, Edna's branch of the Mizells were best known as the proprietors of a sawmill on the south banks of the St. Marys River at a community called Kings Ferry.

Kings Ferry is gone. Though it predates the highway, it would have been west of Interstate 95. Crandall is another lost community on the St. Marys River that would have been east of Interstate 95. At Crandall, the bluffs of which are seen below, E.P. was well known for the sawmill he ran and the cattle he raised with his brothers.

E.P. and Edna had five children, E.P. Jr., Stuart, Barbara, Suzanne, and Kathleen. The family moved to Fernandina when Suzanne was eight. She attended Wesleyan College in Macon before returning to Fernandina and marrying Ira William Hardee in 1944. Ira operated his family's business that sold supplies to local shrimpers. It was known as Standard Marine, and its building is still located on the northwest corner of North Second and Ash Streets.

When Ira died in 1970, Suzanne became vice president of the company. She also directed the local chamber of commerce and ran a local bank. These accomplishments are significant, but they might not be her most lasting legacy.

That would be her contributions to local historic preservation. She was the leader of the Amelia Island–Fernandina Restoration Foundation in its early days when restoration and preservation were at their most pivotal time. After the establishment of the Amelia Island Museum of History, she became an avid volunteer as the museum's archivist. In fact, the room the archives are stored in is now named in her honor. In addition, she authored important books about Fernandina's history, such as *The Golden Age of Amelia Island: A Glimpse*. Suzanne died in 2004. (Opposite, courtesy Susan Steger; below, courtesy Davis family collection.)

Susan Steger

Suzanne had five daughters. One of those is Susan Steger. Having started out in banking, she was elected to the city commission in 2008, and eventually became mayor. In 2012, she cofounded the *Fernandina Observer*, an online news journal. (Courtesy Susan Steger.)

Clyde Davis

Steger's first cousin is local attorney Clyde Davis. He is the son of E.P. Davis Jr., Suzanne Davis Hardee's brother. Clyde has practiced law in Nassau County for over 30 years. He has served as city attorney and board attorney for the Amelia Island Nassau County Association of Realtors and the Ocean Highway and Port Authority. This is his portrait from his senior year at Fernandina Beach High School. (Courtesy Fernandina Beach High School Archives.)

Hardee Brothers

Suzanne Davis Hardee was married to Ira William Hardee, whose father bore the same name. Ira Sr. was one of nine siblings. He, along with two of his brothers, Noble Anthony and John, founded Standard Marine and a hardware store that was eventually in the building pictured here that now houses Fernandina's Fantastic Fudge. Noble Anthony Hardee was married to Emma Love Hardee and is seen on page 38. Their son Will Love Hardee, the oldest child on page 38, is the namesake for Will Hardee Boulevard, a well-traveled local road. The Hardee Brothers Hardware Store at 218 Centre Street is seen here in the 1980s shortly before it closed. (Courtesy Amelia Island Museum of History.)

Bill and Clinch Kavanaugh

Influential brothers Bill and Clinch Kavanaugh are also in the Hardee family tree. Their grandfather was also Ira William Hardee Sr. Clinch, pictured here, is a well-known local attorney. Bill is a harbor pilot by trade. He also has considerable land holdings on the island, especially at Old Town. He lives in the Baker House, seen on page 34, which belonged to his great-great-grandfather Archibald on the other side of the family as the Hardees. (Courtesy Steve Leimberg/UnSeenImages.com.)

Ted Steger Sr.

Susan Steger was married to the late Ted Steger Jr., who was research director for Monsanto. His brother Mack is a local pharmacist who followed in the footsteps of their father, Ted Steger Sr. (pictured). Ted Sr. moved to the island in 1959 from Illinois and opened a pharmacy on Atlantic Avenue. He was a World War II veteran and a member of the Amelia Lodge. (Courtesy Susan Steger.)

Glyndon Waas

Like Mack Steger, Glyndon Waas also took over a drugstore from his father. Waas Drug Co. was a popular drugstore at the northwest corner of Centre and North Sixth Streets. In addition, Waas founded a real estate company that would become Amelia Realty Company, which was quite active in the early days of the Amelia Island Plantation. He was a founding member of the Amelia Island Plantation's Men's Golf Association too. Waas is seen here on the right, as a young man, along with his friend Theo Davis. (Courtesy Amelia Island Museum of History.)

Dr. Kay Johnson
Dr. Kay Johnson graduated from Fernandina Beach High School in 1950, but that was not the end of her time spent in schools. She went on to be a noted professor in the School of Education at Jacksonville University and started a child development center within the university, known as Wilma's Little People School. Dr. Johnson is an important figure in the Duncan Lamont Clinch Historical Society. (Author's collection.)

Millie Campbell
Millie Campbell spent nearly three decades from the late 1960s until 1995 as principal at Southside Elementary. Before becoming principal, the Louisville, Kentucky, native spent time in various educational roles in the school district, including a stint at the Peck School. Campbell was principal at Southside when the district fired a teacher there, Gene Arline, because she was infected with tuberculosis. Arline sued, and the case ended up in the US Supreme Court at the height of the AIDS scare of the mid-1980s. The court ruled in favor of Arline in *School Board of Nassau County v. Arline* stating that a person with an infectious disease may be considered a "handicapped individual" and thus protected under previous laws. (Courtesy Ray family collection.)

Lasserre Family

The Lasserre name is certainly legendary in Fernandina. Charles Lasserre Sr. started the first car dealership in Fernandina. The business sold Fords from a showroom at the southwest corner of Centre and South Fourth Streets where the Amelia Tavern is today. It is pictured opposite at bottom. The dealership was later moved to the northwest corner of Gum and South Eighth Streets and is seen in the aerial view above. At that time, Charles Sr.'s son Gene (opposite top) was president of Lasserre Motor Company. As an Ocean Highway and Port Authority commissioner, he played a key role in the development of the Port of Fernandina, and Gene Lasserre Boulevard in Yulee is named in his honor.

Gene's brother Curtiss (left) opened his own real estate agency in 1976. The prominent agency is operated by various family members, including Curtiss's son Charles. Another son, Jon, is a local attorney. (Courtesy Amelia Island Museum of History.)

Wayne Benner

Coach Wayne Benner grew up in Indiana and enrolled in the Army after graduating from high school. From there, he enrolled in Florida State University and played on the Seminoles football and baseball teams. In 1954, he was hired by Fernandina Beach High School to teach physical education and to coach. He moved to Fernandina Beach Middle School in 1969 and worked there until his retirement in 1983. (Courtesy Fernandina Beach High School Archives.)

Albert "Ybor" Alvarez

Albert Alvarez's life's work was spent as a carpenter at Rayonier in Fernandina Beach. He was born in Ybor City, Florida, and was best known by his nickname "Ybor." Alvarez organized a baseball team for Rayonier that played other teams in the area. Later, he was instrumental in bringing Little League baseball to town. Alvarez spent many years as umpire for the city's Little League and even served as umpire for the 1971 Little League World Series. The city's recreational facility and softball fields off Bailey Road near the airport bear his name. (Courtesy Alvarez family collection.)

Norma Jean Smith

Norma Jean Smith was a player in the local sports scene as well, but not as an athlete. She spent her career working as the coordinator of data processing for the Nassau County School District and worked nights at the iconic Putt Putt Golf Course at Main Beach. Eventually, she purchased the course from Tump Lewis and ran it for 27 years before selling it to Aaron Bean in 2009. He sold it five years later. Smith hosted tournaments on Friday nights that were a favorite event of many locals. She is seen here seated on the left with her daughter Phyllis and grandson Kyle. (Courtesy Lents family collection.)

Claude Haddock

Claude Haddock was known for his musical talents. Born and raised in Fernandina, Haddock's day job was with the postal service; however, he often sang at weddings and was a staple in the choirs of the First Baptist Church, and later, Amelia Baptist Church. He was also involved in several other local choir and singing groups. (Courtesy Haddock family collection.)

Ken Williams
Ken Williams is a Peck High School graduate who went on to a successful career as a songwriter. His Peck High School senior portrait is seen here. Following his graduation, Williams moved to New York, where he has written and collaborated on many well-known songs, like The Main Ingredient's "Everybody Plays the Fool" in 1972. (Courtesy Amelia Island Museum of History.)

Mike Geiger and Woody Mullis
Mike Geiger and Woody Mullis graduated from Fernandina Beach High School (FBHS) a year apart from each other in the mid-1970s. They moved to Nashville and tried their luck in songwriting. The duo has written songs for some of country music's top stars. One song, "Darlene," performed by T. Graham Brown, reached the top of country music's charts in 1988. Mullis and Geiger were named Broadcast Music Inc. songwriters of the year in 1989. Mullis is seen here holding the plaque on the left during his 2007 FBHS Hall of Fame induction. (Author's collection.)

Bill Mason

Bill Mason was inducted into the FBHS Hall of Fame that same year. His son Damon represented him and is seen at the center of the previous photograph. Bill began teaching at FBHS in the 1960s and continued until the mid-1990s. He taught English and music at the school and was known for his colorful personality in the classroom. He started the Madrigals vocal group at the high school and was very involved with music at Memorial United Methodist Church. The Madrigals have since fizzled out but were very well known and used to perform at many local events. (Courtesy Fernandina Beach High School Archives.)

Elizabeth Dressler

Elizabeth "Betty" Dressler was a staple at Fernandina Beach High School from 1961 to 1996. She was born locally and served as a Women Airforce Service Pilot (WASP) during World War II. She taught science, mostly chemistry and physics, at FBHS and was renowned for being among the school's most challenging teachers. Her home was at the southwest corner of North Sixth and Broome Streets. (Courtesy Fernandina Beach High School Archives.)

Ron Sapp

Ron Sapp is a local product and graduated from Fernandina Beach High School in 1965. His next stop was Georgia Military College in Milledgeville, Georgia. He was drafted and served in the US Air Force and was stationed in Germany. He married Kasey Askins, whose parents ran a grocery at South Sixth and Ash Streets.

After the Air Force, Sapp came back to Fernandina, completed college at the University of North Florida on the G.I. Bill, and started writing for a small newspaper called the *Amelia Island Sun*. From there, he worked for Rayonier at its Fernandina mill, then took over a sign-making business his father-in-law also ran.

The sign shop did not appear as though it was going to be an overwhelming success, so when Fernandina Beach High School principal Bill Fryar asked Sapp to join the staff in 1987, he agreed. He spent the next 28 years as a social studies teacher and icon at the school until his retirement in 2015. He was instrumental in the development of the school's Advanced Placement program, teaching US government, economics, and psychology.

Sapp's greatest influence over his hometown though, might be through his involvement with the city commission. He served eight terms as a city commissioner, more than anyone else in the city of Fernandina Beach. (Ben Sorensen served more in the city of Fernandina and Fernandina Beach, before the two were consolidated).

Among his most lasting accomplishments as a city commissioner are the development of the Egans Creek Greenway, the preservation of public beach accesses, and height limits and lot consolidation restrictions along the beach. Sapp has been a supporter of preservation and limited development within the city limits. He continues to keep his hands in local politics, most notably through the column he regularly writes for the Fernandina Beach *News-Leader*. (Author's collection.)

Smiley Lee
Joseph "Smiley" Lee was a lifelong resident of Fernandina who served three terms on the city commission. He operated a salvage company but was involved in other industries like shrimping and real estate. Lee was known for his colorful character. He once brought an alligator to a bar and dumped a truck full of chicken manure at the front door of the *News-Leader*, upset with their political coverage of him. (Courtesy Lee family collection.)

Curtis "Topsy" Smith
Curtis "Topsy" Smith started out as a police officer but was injured in the line of duty in 1972. He opened the Gulf gas station at the southwest corner of Centre and Eighth Streets. Smith was another well-known character who served on the city commission. In that role, he and fellow commissioners John Beckett and Smiley Lee were indicted for requesting bribes. All were convicted, but Lee successfully won an appeal that overturned his conviction. Smith is pictured here on the right with Nick Deonas when both men served on the Ocean Highway and Port Authority. (Courtesy Deonas family collection.)

Grace Butler

Smith was of course removed from the city commission, and Grace Butler was appointed by Gov. Reuben Askew as his replacement in 1973. This made her the first woman to serve on the commission in the history of the town. Her late husband, Gordon, had previously served as mayor. Grace won reelection in 1975 but lost to Charles Albert three years later. Grace also taught elementary school in Fernandina for many years and was very popular in the local community. She is seen second from right at a Shrimp Boat Festival. Others pictured are, from left to right, Denise Hayworth, A.F. Dougherty, Melvin Dougherty, and US senator Richard Stone. (Courtesy City of Fernandina Beach.)

Ray and T-Ray Mullis

There was a time when Topsy Smith's Gulf station was one of only two places to buy gas in town. The other belonged to the Mullis family. Ray Mullis began working with his father at a service station they owned at Main Beach in the 1950s. In 1970, they bought a second station at the southeast corner of South Eighth and Beech Streets. Ray's son T-Ray joined the business in 1988. Ten years later, T-Ray started a small take-out burger restaurant at the gas station. The operation quickly grew into one of Fernandina's most iconic and beloved restaurants. They chose to stop selling gas in 2010, and the building is now exclusively a restaurant, though it still looks more like a service station. (Courtesy T-Ray Mullis.)

Dale Dees

Dale Dees was raised in Fernandina Beach. He served in the Army and returned to Fernandina to establish a dry-cleaning business and gun store on South Eighth Street. Those were operated with his wife, Sharon, for many years. Dees represents another unique personality to serve on the city commission. (Courtesy Dale Dees.)

Beano Roberts

Don "Beano" Roberts was born in New York and moved to Fernandina in 1952. He managed the Ilan Theatre, once located on the northwest corner of Atlantic Avenue and North Eleventh Street. He also owned the Ocean View Motel. In addition to those businesses, Roberts has worked as a local realtor and teacher and is highly regarded for his involvement with civic affairs, including 10 years as a city commissioner with a stint as mayor. He has served on various advisory boards and worked on the Shrimp Festival Committee throughout its history. (Courtesy Beano Roberts.)

Charles Albert

Charles Albert is among the most renowned members of Fernandina's African American community. He grew up in Nassauville, actually at a small complex known as Goffinsville, built by a Russian immigrant named Saul Goffin, owner of an oyster cannery there. Goffin employed many African Americans to gather oysters from the Nassau River. Albert's father was one of those men but later took a job at Rayonier.

Charles attended a one-room school in the Goffinsville area until black schools were consolidated, and he continued his education at Peck High School, graduating in 1949. He next went to Edward Waters College in Jacksonville. In 1953, he was drafted into the Army and spent two years stationed in Japan. When he returned, he continued his college education at Florida A&M University and graduated in 1959.

Albert briefly worked at the Florida School for Boys in Marianna but soon came back to Fernandina as a teacher at Peck High School. When desegregation came in the late 1960s, he transferred to Fernandina Beach Junior High School. In all, he taught for more than 30 years before his retirement from the Nassau County School System.

As a member of the Peck High School faculty during desegregation, Albert played a role in that process. He helped organize a Little League and Pop Warner League that put local children of different races on the same teams. This placed young people together working for a common purpose, which greatly reduced or even eliminated strife in Fernandina. As a teacher, Albert was aware that good communication with all school stakeholders was crucial in making desegregation work and played an active role in those types of discussions.

Charles Albert is also known for his role in city politics. He served as a city commissioner for 18 years, including multiple terms as mayor. In fact, he was the first and currently only African American to serve as mayor of the City of Fernandina Beach. (Courtesy Steve Leimberg/UnSeenImages.com.)

Franz and Martha Lee Mitchell
Franz and Martha Lee Mitchell are a much-beloved Fernandina couple. Martha Lee's father, Gene Barnhardt, owned Gene's, which opened as "The Biggest Little Store in Town" in 1951. It sold just about everything, including tobacco products, magazines, soda, televisions, and bicycles. Franz and Martha Lee married in 1958, and when Gene died in 1961, the young couple took over. Franz opened a bookstore, Mitchell's Books and Things, on Centre Street in 1975. Martha Lee also taught in the local schools for many years, mostly at Emma Love Hardee Elementary. They are seen here in front of the bookstore following the "blizzard" of 1989. (Courtesy Kitty Morris.)

Bob and Melba Whitaker
Robison's Jewelry Co. was established in the Swann Building in 1952. Bob Whitaker came to Fernandina Beach a few years later from North Carolina to work at one of the paper mills. In 1966, he bought Robison's Jewelry. In 1973, Whitaker and Franz Mitchell purchased the Angel Building at the northwest corner of Centre and North Third Streets, which at the time was a five-and-dime store. They split the building in two: half was Mitchell's Books and Things, the other half was the new Robison's Jewelry, owned by Whitaker. Bob's wife, Melba, also worked as a popular teacher. The Whitakers have long been important figures in the Historic Fernandina Business Association and helped to lead the revitalization efforts of Centre Street in the late 1970s. The Whitakers' sons Brett and Jeff now operate the jewelry store. (Courtesy Paige Whitaker.)

Aubrey Williams

Aubrey Williams spent the last half of his childhood in Fernandina. After graduating from the University of Florida, he spent time working for the Container Corporation, and the company moved him from Fernandina to Chicago. Eventually, Williams made his way back to Fernandina and joined his father's company, Land and Williams Inc. The company was best known as the holder of nearly all the liquor licenses in town for a time during the last half of the 20th century. Their holdings included Florida's oldest bar, the Palace Saloon, and Williams can take credit for the creation of Pirate's Punch, Fernandina's signature drink. Williams was also instrumental in the development of the Oyster Bay subdivision. (Courtesy Williams family collection.)

George Sheffield

George Sheffield is a third-generation local. He has spent the majority of his career selling insurance through his company Amelia Underwriters Inc. In 2003, he purchased the Palace Saloon. Working with his son Wes, Sheffield added other local bars, restaurants, and even a golf course to his portfolio. Today, the Amelia Island Hospitality Group dominates the nightlife and other opportunities for tourist activities on Amelia Island. Sheffield is also passionate about local historic preservation and promotion of downtown commerce. (Courtesy George Sheffield.)

Arthur Simmons

Arthur Simmons was better known as the Ox Man. His ox's name was Billy, and Simmons raised him from a calf. In the 1950s and 1960s, Billy would pull Simmons around town in the cart, pictured here, as Simmons rummaged through garbage cans looking for scraps to sell or use. (Courtesy Amelia Island Museum of History.)

Felix Jones

There might not be a local more legendary or at least more beloved than Felix Jones. Jones grew up in Fernandina and regularly rides his tricycle around downtown while playing his harmonica and selling things such as newspapers, whole pineapples, and food his mother prepares, like boiled peanuts. In 2009, Jones was found to be in violation of an ordinance against mobile street vending. Locals came en masse to a city commission meeting to support him, and he was allowed to continue his activities. (Author's collection.)

Bean Family

The Bean family is among the most abundant and well-known families on the island. Lewis, or "Red," and Joan Bean first moved to Fernandina from Kentucky in 1950. Red was hired as a shop teacher for the local schools and coached multiple sports. When the couple first came to the island, they lived in a home that was east of the area that is now home to the Elizabeth Pointe Lodge. It has long since been washed away by the ocean.

Joan started teaching dance to local children in 1953. She began her lessons at the school associated with St. Michael's Catholic Church. Over time, her "studio" had stops at the Keystone Hotel, Atlantic Avenue Recreation Center, and the couple's home on North Fifteenth Street. In 1986, Bean School of Dance opened a dedicated formal studio on North Third Street that is still in business.

Red and Joan had nine children whose births span almost two decades. Diane directed special education for Nassau County Schools for many years. Daughter Drue and sons Gary and Steve are involved with pharmaceuticals. Mark, Mason, and Warren are each involved in building, real estate, and building maintenance. David works for Rayonier.

Youngest child Aaron is notable in his own right. He graduated from Jacksonville University and started out in local banking. In 1996, he launched his political life with his election to the Fernandina Beach city commission. He went on to serve as mayor. In 2000, he was elected to the Florida House of Representatives and won a seat in the state senate in 2012.

Red Bean passed away in 1989, but he and Joan have 18 grandchildren and a number of great-grandchildren. The entire family, including spouses, is seen here on the occasion of Joan's 90th birthday in 2016. She is seen in the center of the picture with glasses. Aaron is standing on the far right. (Courtesy Bean family collection.)

Rodeffer Family

The Rodeffers are another prominent family in town. Their patriarch was Bill Rodeffer, who was born in Pennsylvania in 1920. After serving in the Merchant Marines during World War II, he attended dental school in Virginia. After that, he moved to Fernandina and opened a practice that would last 55 years. "Doc," as he was often known, served on the local school board for 20 years and was a longtime member of the local Kiwanis Club and key member of the chamber of commerce.

Bill's wife, Aline, was also highly respected throughout the community, mostly for her generosity and kindness. Together, the couple were a pillar of First Baptist Church for many years. They had five children. David and Jimmy are educators and administrators in Nassau County Schools. Joe works in the sales of building materials. Henry is a well-respected local physician. He is a member of the Fernandina Beach High School Hall of Fame along with his sister Suellen. She practices orthodontics locally along with her husband, Tod Garner. Their practice leads the area in the orthodontics field. (Courtesy Rodeffer family collection.)

Mary Duffy

During the summer months, a team of volunteers head out in the morning hours to walk the beaches of Amelia Island in search of fresh sea turtle nests. When they find them, they are marked and protected. This team is the Amelia Island Sea Turtle Watch, headed by Mary Duffy. Duffy served as assistant principal at Fernandina Beach High School for many years and as director of student services for the Nassau County School District. She poses here in front of a turtle nest on the beach. (Author's collection.)

Joel Stockstill

Joel Stockstill came to Fernandina Beach from Kentucky to coach the FBHS Football team. He coached for 12 years before leaving the sidelines in the late 1980s. However, he remained a guidance counselor at the school until 2008. Stockstill coached some of the school's best all-time players like Terrence Flagler. He also coached his sons Jeff and Rick at the school. Jeff went on to start at quarterback for Florida State University, and Rick has proven to be a successful college football coach. Joel is pictured here (first row, center) with the 1985 Pirates football team. (Courtesy Fernandina Beach High School Archives.)

Ken Roland

Ken Roland is a legendary coach at FBHS as well. He started coaching the baseball team in 1983 and has amassed over 600 wins. Roland grew up in Fernandina and attended the school himself. He has taught business education at the school and served as athletic director. Many of his players have earned area awards and gone on to play and coach in college and professional leagues. He is seen here (first row, far right) with his 2003 players, who were runners-up for the state championship. (Courtesy Fernandina Beach High School Archives.)

Jon Shave

Jon Shave is arguably the best baseball player the community has ever produced. He is the grandson of Judge Thomas Shave (see page 61). Jon graduated from Fernandina Beach High School in 1986 as an All-American. He played college ball at Mississippi State before being drafted in the fifth round by the Texas Rangers in 1990. He played three seasons in the Major Leagues as an infielder for the Rangers and Minnesota Twins as well as other seasons in the minor leagues. (Courtesy Fernandina Beach High School Archives.)

Terrence Flagler
If Jon Shave is the best baseball player Fernandina ever produced, surely Terrance Flagler is the best football player. At Fernandina Beach High School, he excelled in football and basketball. He received a football scholarship to Clemson University, where he played running back. His senior year there, he was an All-American and led the Atlantic Coast Conference in rushing. He was drafted in the first round by the San Francisco 49ers and won two Super Bowls with them. Flagler remained in the NFL for five years. He is pictured here escorting Patricia Davis at the 1981 FBHS Homecoming. (Courtesy Fernandina Beach High School Archives.)

Max Hord
Max Hord is another accomplished athlete. He started boxing as a young boy, switched to baseball during high school, then went back to boxing upon graduation from Fernandina Beach High School. His most notable fight came in 1979 against Tony Danza, who would soon quit boxing to concentrate on acting. The two fought in Madison Square Garden. Danza knocked out Hord in the first round. (Courtesy Amelia Island Museum of History.)

92

Bill Leeper

Bill Leeper was another great
athlete from Fernandina Beach
High School. He played catcher
for the Pirates and was drafted by
the New York Mets in 1971. His
baseball days were short lived, but
he has been a valuable member of
the Fernandina Beach community.
He has served as mayor of the
city and sheriff of Nassau County.
He and his wife, Emma, also own
and operate Corner-Copia, an
established gift and novelty store
on Centre Street. (Courtesy
Bill Leeper.)

Granville "Doc" Burgess

Doc Burgess was synonymous
with the court system in town for
many years. He was a private civil
law attorney before transitioning
into a prosecutor with the state
attorney's office. In 2006, he was
elected Nassau County judge
for the Fourth Judicial Circuit, a
position he held until his death
in 2012. (Courtesy Burgess
family collection.)

Arthur "Buddy" Jacobs

Buddy Jacobs grew up in Fernandina with a somewhat challenging childhood but overcame that to attend the University of Florida (UF), where he served as student body president during the 1966–1967 school year. Jacobs worked for some time at UF, completed law school, and returned to Fernandina in 1972. For years, he lived in downtown Fernandina Beach at Villa las Palmas. Jacobs has worked as a controversial attorney and lobbyist in town throughout his career. (Courtesy Amelia Island Museum of History.)

David and Kim Page

Husband and wife David and Kim Page are both local products. Kim is a respected attorney and served on the city commission in the 1990s. David is a family physician. He maintains his own practice and volunteers his time with the Samaritan Clinic run by the Barnabas Center. His parents ran a dairy and nursery in Yulee, the namesake of Page's Dairy Road. (Courtesy Kim Page.)

Dr. Bailey Dickens

Dr. Henry Bailey Dickens was born and raised in Central Georgia. He graduated from the Medical College of Georgia and eventually made his way to Fernandina, where he opened a family medical practice in 1941. He was among the best-known physicians in town until his retirement in 1991. (Courtesy Bray family collection.)

Wesley Poole

Wesley Poole spent his childhood locally. After stops at Florida State University and the University of Florida, he was admitted to the Florida Bar in 1974. He served a stint in the US Air Force as a staff judge advocate before establishing a private practice in Fernandina in 1978. He has taught at what is now Florida State College in Jacksonville and served on the board of trustees there. Poole has served as city attorney and was appointed Nassau County judge by Gov. Rick Scott in 2013 following the death of Granville "Doc" Burgess. (Courtesy Wesley Poole.)

Chris Hall Bryan
Chris Bryan's father started the Florida Petroleum Corp., which initially provided fuel to local shrimp boats but expanded exponentially in time. Chris eventually took over ownership of the company. As an alumna of the University of Florida, she is an avid Florida Gators fan and longtime booster. She was inducted into the inaugural class of the Fernandina Beach High School Hall of Fame. (Author's collection.)

Johnny Myers
Johnny Myers is among the town's most successful entrepreneurs. He moved to Fernandina Beach as a child and graduated from FBHS in 1965. He enlisted in the Air Force before returning to Fernandina. He became involved in a family grocery store on South Eighth Street, and later entered the shrimping business when he acquired two boats. His next venture involved tractors. Myers started out assisting local farmers, but the business expanded to industrial purposes. From that, Myers Tree Service, which is his most visible operation today, was born. Myers has also been involved in real estate development such as the Ocean Breeze subdivision off South Fourteenth Street. He is seen here at his FBHS Hall of Fame induction. (Author's collection.)

Pat Gass and Steve Kelley

Pat Gass and Steve Kelley first came to Fernandina in 1966 as children when their father, Rev. Ralph Kelley, was appointed rector at St. Peters Episcopal Church. Over time, Pat, who is pictured here, has worked at various local businesses and the port authority. In 2012, she was elected to the city commission.

Steve Kelley is also well known locally. He operated Kelley Pest Control for almost 30 years before retiring from day-to-day operations. Kelley is involved in the Shriners and Optimist Club and has served as a county commissioner. (Courtesy Pat Gass.)

McCarthy Brothers

Kevin, Brian, and Sean McCarthy are each legendary locals in their own right. They are the sons of the late Harlin and Alice McCarthy, who moved their family to Fernandina Beach from Gloucester, Massachusetts, in 1968. Kevin worked in town as a building contractor for most of his career. In 2000, he created Amelia River Cruises and Charters, which offers boat tours of the Amelia River and Cumberland Sound.

Sean works as a charter boat captain and often serves as a guide on Kevin's tours. He is best known as one of the island's favorite musicians. Something of a local Jimmy Buffet, Sean has recorded professionally in Nashville and can regularly be found providing live entertainment at area restaurants and bars.

Another brother, Brian, ran what is perhaps Fernandina Beach's most memorable restaurants. The Down Under was located underneath the Thomas J. Shave Bridge. It opened in 1980 but closed in 2007. A favorite of locals and tourists from Georgia, the restaurant sat on the Intracoastal Waterway and was famous for its fried shrimp. There are two other siblings in the McCarthy clan, brother Glenn and sister Kerry. Pictured here are, from left to right, Kevin, Brian, Glenn, and Sean. (Courtesy Noah French.)

Charles Fraser

There are very few people who have been as influential to Amelia Island as Charles Fraser, especially for someone who never really lived here. He grew up in Hinesville, Georgia, and graduated from the University of Georgia. The summer following his graduation, he worked for a company partially held by his father that was in the process of harvesting timber from the forest that dominated Hilton Head Island in South Carolina. Fraser became enchanted with the island and convinced his father to give him an interest in the land after the timber was gone.

Fraser attended Yale Law School next, but Hilton Head was never far from his mind. After he graduated, he established the Sea Pines Company, which sold its first lots on Hilton Head in 1957. Hotels and golf courses followed, and to say that Fraser was successful in developing Sea Pines Plantation would be an understatement.

After Hilton Head, Fraser developed resort communities in Virginia, North Carolina, and Puerto Rico. He held most of Cumberland Island and was set to develop it. However, political pressure to keep the island undeveloped eventually persuaded him to donate his holdings to the National Park Foundation.

Fraser had purchased most of the southern end of Amelia Island from the Union Carbide Company in 1970. They had intended to strip mine the area for titanium but realized that project would not be as profitable as they had hoped. Luckily, the Sea Pines Company was an eager buyer as the Cumberland project was falling apart.

In 1972, Fraser unveiled his master plan for Amelia Island Plantation. The focus of the resort was to be "in harmony with nature," so the preservation of creeks, dunes, and the sprawling oak trees was emphasized in planning. Unfortunately, by 1976, the Amelia Island Plantation was bankrupt and was sold to Richard Cooper Investments.

The Sea Pines Company had financial difficulties at some of its other developments as well, and Fraser left the company in 1983. He was killed in a boating accident in the Caribbean in 2002. Amelia Island Plantation was more or less successful, though not necessarily under Fraser's watch. What Fraser did, however, was put the island on the map as a major vacation destination in the South. The Ritz Carlton came along in the early 1990s to solidify that distinction, but the modern tourist industry on Amelia Island was sparked by the vision of Charles Fraser.

Fraser is pictured opposite, as well as a party at the Beach Club, which was the heart of Amelia Island Plantation when the resort first opened. (Courtesy Wood family collection.)

Jack Healan

Jack Healan had worked as vice president and controller of the Sea Pines Company on Hilton Head Island. Richard Cooper brought him to Amelia Island in 1978, and he served in several capacities for the Amelia Island Plantation Company, including chief financial officer, executive vice president, and general manager. In 1990, he took over as president and held that office until 2010, when Omni Hotels and Resorts took over the property.

Healan is a product of Rock Hill, South Carolina, and a Citadel graduate. He fought with the Marines in Vietnam and is also a licensed pilot. In fact, he worked as a corporate pilot and flight instructor prior to his involvement with the Sea Pines Company. He has been as important to life on Amelia's south end as anyone during its entire history. He played a critical role in the Amelia Island Plantation's expansion, development, and establishment as one of the premiere resorts in the Southeast.

As head of the resort, Healan can boast a long list of awards including Florida Hotel and Motel Association's hotelier of the year in 1991, and the 2003 American Hotel and Lodging Association's Lawson A. Odde Award for outstanding contributions to the advancement of the lodging industry. He served in the leadership of both of those groups as well as numerous other industry organizations. In 1992, he was appointed by Gov. Lawton Chiles to the Florida Commission on Tourism and was eventually elected vice-chairman. He attended a White House conference in 1995 on travel tourism as a congressionally appointed delegate. That same year, Healan was inducted into the Florida Tourism Hall of Fame.

Locally, Healan is a past president of the Amelia Island–Fernandina Beach Chamber of Commerce and has been a member of the Nassau County Tourist Development Council since it began. He is on the advisory board of multiple banks and has been a member of the board of directors of Baptist Medical Center, Nassau. (Courtesy Laura Coggin.)

Ralph and Steve Simmons

Brothers Ralph and Steve Simmons grew up on a farm near Statesboro, Georgia. They were both instrumental in the boom that followed the resorts coming to Amelia Island. Ralph had worked with the Sea Pines Company and came to Amelia in 1971. Eventually, he was named vice president of Amelia Island Plantation. He served on the board of the St. Johns River Water Management District and led efforts to preserve land along the St. Marys River near Hilliard. That area is now a state park that bears his name. Ralph passed away in 1996.

Steve followed his brother to the island and opened Fernandina Beach Realty in 1974. Over the years, Steve and his company developed many of the area's residential communities as well as oceanfront condominiums and homes. He has been a deacon at First Baptist Church for more than 30 years where he and his wife, Pam, of 42 years, remain very active. Together, the brothers were ardent outdoorsmen. Ralph is seen on the right with the results of a fishing trip, and Steve is pictured below with his catch from a different trip. (Both, courtesy Simmons family collection.)

Marcy and Jay Mock
Marcy Mock and her son Jay are leaders in local real estate. Marcy built her livelihood as an authority on high-end real estate around the south end's resorts and Summer Beach. Jay, along with his business partner Harry Travett, has been more of a leader on the development side. He has completed residential projects like Highland Dunes and Shell Cove as well as commercial projects like Lofton Square in Yulee and Executive Park in Fernandina. Jay has been involved with the founding and acquisition of local banks too. (Author's collection.)

Richard Cooper
Richard Cooper bought Amelia Island Plantation from Charles Fraser when the Sea Pines Company ran into financial trouble. Thus, he was a key figure in the dawning of a new era, the resort era, on Amelia Island. Cooper expanded operations at the south end of the island with additions like the resort's conference center, Long Point Golf Club, and Osprey Village. (Courtesy Cooper family collection.)

Bill Warner

Bill Warner lives in Jacksonville but has impacted Amelia Island. He founded the Concours d'Elegance held annually at the Ritz Carlton Amelia Island. He started the classic automobile show in 1996 and added an auction three years later. It is now considered one of the world's premiere car shows. Proceeds from the event support local charities like Community Hospice of Northeast Florida. Warner is an automobile enthusiast, businessman, and writer/photographer for *Road & Track* magazine. (Courtesy Bill Warner.)

Les DeMerle

Les DeMerle was invited to Amelia Island to open the Ritz Carlton in 1991. He and his wife, vocalist Bonnie Eisele, initially were regular entertainers at the hotel until 2001. Over time, DeMerle has become synonymous with Amelia Island music. He founded and directs the Amelia Island Jazz Festival, which brings world-class concerts to the area and provides jazz scholarships. The Grammy Award–winning modern jazz drummer is a native of New York and has toured and recorded with greats like Harry James, Wayne Newton, Frank Sinatra, Lou Rawls, and others. (Courtesy Les DeMerle.)

Marsha Dean Phelts
The relationship between the resorts at the south end of the island and property owners at American Beach has had contentious moments. In the 1990s, Amelia Island Plantation had property rights and planned an expansion into American Beach. As an American Beach historian, Marsha Dean Phelts knows that story and others well. She grew up in Jacksonville and worked as a librarian there. She now lives at American Beach and has become one of the leading historians of the community. She has published multiple books about the area. (Courtesy Steve Leimberg/UnSeenImages.com.)

Neil Frink
Neil Frink knows his local African American history too. He has served as president of the A.L. Lewis Historical Society and has chaired the Association for the Study and Preservation of African American History in Nassau County. He grew up in Old Town as his father worked at the nearby Pogey Plant and was the first African American to be a licensed boat captain in Florida. The younger Frink worked in Philadelphia in the automotive manufacturing business but returned to Amelia Island upon his retirement and is a leader in the promotion of local African American History. (Courtesy Steve Leimberg/UnSeenImages.com.)

MaVynee Betsch

MaVynee Betsch was best known simply as the Beach Lady. She was born in 1935 to John Thomas Betsch and Mary Frances Lewis Betsch and was the granddaughter of Abraham Lincoln Lewis. She grew up as a privileged child in Jacksonville and attended the Conservatory at Oberlin College in Ohio. She graduated from there in 1955 with degrees in voice and piano.

Upon her college graduation, she moved to Europe to sing in the German opera. She returned to Jacksonville after seven years and soon moved to American Beach. At that point, she became synonymous with the small community. Betsch founded the American Beach Historical Society and gave tours of the area. She was an ardent environmentalist and fought hard for the preservation of American Beach.

Florida's tallest dune, named Nana, is at American Beach. Betsch succeeded in having ownership of the dune transferred to the National Park System. This also helped provide a buffer between American Beach and the resort development to the immediate south. This worked toward maintaining American Beach as a unique and treasured community, a key part of Betsch's work. She spent her life's savings and inheritance on efforts like these and others.

Betsch was also known for her long dreadlocks and fingernails. Her dreadlocks might have been seven feet long, and she often carried them over her arm like one might carry a purse. She placed buttons that bore sayings or slogans throughout her hair. Most of the sayings were political. She kept the nails of her right hand cut short, but the nails of her left hand were a couple feet long and curled. She kept the type of bag a newspaper might come in over them for protection. Her attire included many bracelets as well as necklaces and rings she might have made herself using things like shells or bones she collected at the beach. Her clothing was usually colorful and often fell off her shoulders—usually, some breezy look that fit a person called the Beach Lady very well.

This look made Betsch instantly recognizable around town. She enjoyed teaching anyone who would listen about the history of American Beach and the need to preserve it. She died in 2005. A couple of months following her death she was honored by the Dalai Lama as an Unsung Hero of Compassion. (Courtesy Amelia Island Museum of History.)

John Cotner

The development of the island's south end brought a wave of new people to town. John Cotner was one of these. He first came to Amelia Island from Atlanta in 1980 to oversee a couple of projects at Amelia Island Plantation as an architect. He did not intend to stay, but ended up starting his own firm. Cotner has performed an array of architectural services locally, from the design of upscale oceanfront homes to historic preservation efforts. He has also sat on many local boards and organizations like the city's parks and recreation advisory committee, Nassau Builders Council, the county construction board of adjustments and appeals, and the St. Peters Episcopal Church Vestry. (Courtesy Steve Leimberg/UnSeenImages.com.)

Anne Coonrod

Anne Coonrod came to Amelia Island in 1974 with her husband to start an architectural business. However, other investment opportunities brought her to the development of Amelia Seafood and a gift store called Front and Centre. Both businesses have been staples of the city waterfront for years. Coonrod's impact on the community reaches far beyond that though. She was a founding member of Micah's Place and the Amelia Island Chamber Music Festival and has been involved in numerous other local business and residential projects. (Courtesy Steve Leimberg/ UnSeenImages.com.)

Asa and Nick Gillette
Brothers Asa and Nick Gillette were raised in Fernandina Beach. They both attended the University of Florida and returned to their hometown to establish an engineering firm. Gillette and Associates opened in 2002 and has grown into a leading design company in the area. The Gillettes have completed a multitude of projects on the island and beyond. (Courtesy Gillette family collection.)

Joel Embry
Joel Embry grew up in Quincy, Florida, but moved to Fernandina Beach in 1979. He has had a long occupation in banking and real estate. He has contributed to Centre Street by working to repurpose historic buildings. However, he is best known as the head developer of Amelia Park, a mixed-use "new urbanism" development at the heart of town. (Courtesy Florida State University.)

Jack Heard

Jack Heard took over Oxley Mortuary, now Oxley-Heard Funeral Directors, in 1974. He acquired the business from Margaret Pickett Oxley. Her husband, Joseph McCall Oxley, started it in 1931 in a home behind First Presbyterian Church. In 1948, it was moved to the historic and picturesque John Denham Palmer House on Atlantic Avenue. Heard bought the house and business after his local contacts made him aware of its availability. (Author's collection.)

Steve Colwell
Steve Colwell grew up in Michigan and perfected the art of candy and fudge making at his parents' store there. In 1989, he came to Amelia Island and opened Fernandina's Fantastic Fudge on Centre Street. The store has grown to be perhaps the most iconic business downtown, and Colwell can regularly be found hand-crafting fudge and candy inside. (Author's collection.)

Patricia Toundas
One of the town's most iconic restaurants is the Marina Restaurant at the foot of Centre Street in Major Duryee's old offices. It was established by the Toundas family, who were primarily shrimpers. Patricia Toundas is the leader of the restaurant's operations. She can usually be found at the eatery's front table holding sway over employees and customers alike. The restaurant is quite popular with locals and hosts some very frequent regulars. (Author's collection.)

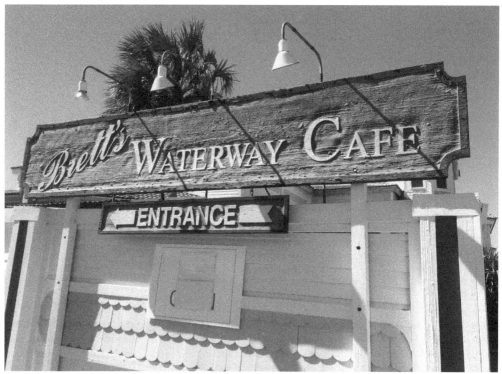

Brett Carter

Brett Carter came to Amelia Island from Tennessee in 1984. Since then, he has been a highly successful restaurateur with multiple restaurants, most notably Brett's Waterway Cafe, seen here and featured at the Fernandina Beach waterfront. Along with his partner Robert "Tip" Fisher, Carter also deals in antiques and fine furniture. (Author's collection.)

Terry Lacoss

Fishing, of course, is a popular activity around Fernandina. Terry Lacoss is one of Amelia Island's charter boat captains who takes others out into the surrounding waters to fish. He organized the Amelia Island Charter Boat Association in 1991. His own charter boat business began long before that though. In addition to fishing, Lacoss has owned the Amelia Angler, a local sportfishing supply and apparel store, since 1978. Lacoss can boast many fishing awards and local records. He is seen in the foreground of this photograph. (Courtesy Terry Lacoss.)

Chuck Hall

Chuck Hall has deep roots in Fernandina. His great-grandfather served as the county judge, his grandfather ran a local store that catered to the many ships coming in and out of port, and his father worked at the Rayonier Mill. Hall conducts multiple operations via the internet. He is also actively involved in community affairs, specifically those downtown, and is an important contributor to the Historic Fernandina Business Association and the Amelia Island–Fernandina Restoration Foundation. He is pictured speaking to the crowd at a local event. (Author's collection.)

Tim Poynter

Tim Poynter moved to Fernandina Beach in 2000. The Cincinnati, Ohio, product made short work in executing his business savvy. By 2012, he dominated North Third Street with his popular restaurants Café Karibo and Timoti's Fry Shack. Café Karibo also includes the successful Karibrew, which brews small batch beers. Poynter has served as a city commissioner, and his son Sean is a world champion stand-up paddle boarder. (Author's collection.)

Don Shaw
Don Shaw is a native of Canada. He moved to the United States in 1955, and job-related circumstances placed him on the ground floor of the coin laundry industry that soon exploded. He retired to Amelia Island in 1995. Through his local company Cambridge South Inc., Shaw collected buildings in downtown Fernandina Beach and on Centre Street. In 2000, he constructed the building at 107 Centre Street for his bookstore, Books Plus. He eventually sold the store. It moved and later closed, but the building is still known as the Shaw Building. (Author's collection.)

Johnny Miller
Johnny Miller has served as a Fernandina Beach city commissioner and mayor. He tends bar at the Palace Saloon and claims to have the city's largest working desk there. Miller was born in Washington, DC, and spent much of his childhood in Atlanta. He served 20 years in the Navy and moved to Fernandina in 2006. The ardent environmentalist has also worked for the city as a lifeguard. (Author's collection.)

Dave Voorhes
Dave Voorhes is better known as Pajama Dave. He has an affinity for pajama pants. He often wore them to work his jobs in construction, as a charter boat captain, or as he rode around town on his motorcycle. Eventually locals took notice of his unusual dress, and the nickname grew from there. That led to his development of Pajama Life, his own line of pajamas, which are sold online and in his Fernandina Beach store. (Author's collection.)

Robin Lentz
Robin Lentz arrived in Fernandina Beach in 2002 and began teaching in the public schools. She is best known for her civic roles, however, and has served on the board of Big Brother Big Sisters, Relay for Life, and Amelia Island Montessori School. These propelled her to a city commission seat in 2014, and later, the mayor's chair. Lentz is also an avid runner and an important member of the Amelia Island Runners Club. (Courtesy Robin Lentz.)

Donna Paz Kaufman
Lentz was involved in the 2014–2015 Fernandina Beach Library improvements. Donna Paz Kaufman was as well. After moving to Fernandina in 2002 with her husband, Mark, she was quickly elected president of Friends of the Library. Her efforts to improve the local library resulted in her receiving the Barbara Kingsolver/Friends of the Library USA Award and the Florida Library Association Award for Library Advocacy. Paz Kaufman operates a business that offers training to bookstore owners. (Courtesy Steve Leimberg/UnSeenImages.com.)

Ron Kurtz
Ron Kurtz moved to Fernandina over 20 years ago and quickly established himself as an important part of the community. He is a valued contributor to the Fernandina Little Theatre, most notably as a director. He has written books about the island and has served on several local boards. (Courtesy Steve Leimberg/UnSeenImages.com.)

Janice Ancrum

Janice Ancrum's current position is executive director of the Council on Aging. She has decades of experience working with local groups and nonprofit agencies, including the United Way, Girls Scouts of America, YMCA, and Barnabas Center. (Courtesy Janice Ancrum.)

Aaron Morgan

Aaron Morgan moved to Fernandina Beach in 2004. He began working professionally as a pilot, but has left his mark on the island through efforts related to local parks. Morgan saw the need for a universally accessible playground and worked tirelessly to raise funds and recruit volunteers through his nonprofit 8 Flags Playscapes. Those efforts brought about the 2014 opening of Pirate Playground behind the Atlantic Avenue Recreation Center. Morgan followed that with a revitalization of the Egans Creek Park. (Author's collection.)

Brandy Carvalho

Brandy Carvalho is a leader in Nassau County nonprofits. She grew up locally and graduated from the University of Florida with advanced degrees from Florida Gulf Coast University and Utah State University. She formerly served as executive director of the Nassau Humane Society and has worked with Micah's Place and the Museum of Science and History in Jacksonville. Carvalho has a passion for animals and is involved with the White Oak Conservation Foundation and the animal sanctuary, established by the late paper magnate Howard Gilman. (Courtesy Brandy Carvalho.)

Jason Mudd

Jason Mudd graduated from Fernandina Beach High School in 1994, followed by the University of Missouri's prestigious School of Journalism. He worked in public relations in various capacities before founding Axia Public Relations in 2002, which is now a leading PR firm. Mudd spent his career advising some of America's most admired brands. He has since won accolades including Emmy awards and recognition from *PRWeek* as a rising star. Mudd was instrumental in raising funds for the city's first public skate park at Main Beach. He lives on Amelia Island with his wife and two children. (Courtesy Jason Mudd.)

Mac Morriss

Mac Morriss is a tireless volunteer and has given countless hours of his time to organizations like Joy to the Children, Builders Care of Nassau County, and 8 Flags Playscapes. He won the 2012 Elsie Harper Award for Nassau County Volunteer of the Year. He also plays a new and important local role as the age of social media has brought change to town. Several local groups now exist on social media that dominate the way the community discusses local issues and shares local information. Morriss is the administrator of one of these influential groups, Facebook's Amelia Island Fernandina Beach Network. (Author's collection.)

John Drew

John Drew has contributed to local nonprofits as a founding father of Micah's Place, which aids victims of domestic violence. He was appointed Nassau County tax collector by Gov. Jeb Bush in 2006 to replace Gwen Miller, and subsequently won reelection. He has served as president of the Florida Tax Collectors Association and as a member of state-level organizations. Drew grew up in Fernandina Beach and graduated from FBHS in 1991. (Courtesy John Drew.)

Frank Ofeldt

Frank Ofeldt started coming to Amelia Island from his hometown in Ocala in his early years to volunteer with Fort Clinch's living history program. He took a job at Fort Clinch State Park in 1994 and is one of the island's most knowledgeable historians, especially in the area of military affairs. Ofeldt continues to participate in the fort's living history program, portraying a Civil War–era Union soldier occupying the fort in the early 1860s. (Courtesy Steve Leimberg/UnSeenImages.com.)

Mike and Jennifer Harrison

Mike and Jennifer Harrison are natives of England. A camping trip at Fort Clinch led them to the discovery of Old Town and the purchase of two lots there. Several years later in 2001 they built a house and have been championing the island's small, original settlement ever since. They maintain a website about Old Town and led efforts to celebrate its bicentennial in 2011. The Harrisons are involved in several local organizations and historic preservation efforts. (Courtesy Steve Leimberg/UnSeenImages.com.)

Tae Rho

Dr. Tae Rho came to Amelia Island from South Korea after a short time in New York. He is a graduate of Kyungpook National University College of Medicine in Daegu, South Korea. Rho practiced pediatrics locally for over 40 years. Now retired, he was known for his seemingly endless availability and impeccable work ethic. Rho regularly saw patients in his office at odd hours and on weekends and seldom missed a birth at the local hospital. (Courtesy Tae Rho.)

Marlene Deutcher

Marlene Deutcher is widely known locally as "Miss Marlene." The Canadian native moved to town in 1981 from Montreal. She worked at the local library in the children's department and provided art lessons. Indeed, teaching art to children is her passion. She has hosted summer camps and is the art director for Amelia Island Montessori School. She is involved with the Amelia Island Art Association and Memorial United Methodist Church as well. (Author's collection.)

Sean McGill

Sean McGill and McGill Aviation are synonymous with local aviation today. McGill graduated from Hawaii Pacific University, where he owned several scuba businesses before following his father to Amelia Island. His father sought to become a fixed-based operator (FBO) for an airport at a resort destination. Sean now runs that FBO. He also actively participates in triathlons and has worked to bring those events to Amelia Island. (Courtesy Sean McGill.)

Thea Seagraves

Thea Seagraves has ties to aviation as well. Her father was in the Air Force, and Thea spent her childhood in the Far East, where the family was stationed. She arrived in Fernandina with her husband in 2003. Seagraves is an avid volunteer and talented storyteller. She is well known for her work through the Amelia Island Museum of History. (Courtesy Steve Leimberg/UnSeenImages.com.)

Joe Palmer

A Waycross, Georgia, native, Joe Palmer came to Fernandina Beach in 1986 to cover the local beat for the *Florida Times Union*. He was lured away to Tampa in 1997 to work for the Florida Public Defender's Office as an investigator. He spent time in the same capacity for the federal government and even operated independently as a private investigator for a while. He returned to Fernandina in 2005 and began writing a popular column for the *News-Leader*, "A Cup of Joe." He occasionally does some freelance writing as well. (Courtesy Joe Palmer.)

Andrew and Cara Curtin

Cara Curtin is a retired naval officer who also writes regularly for the *News-Leader*. She has written several novels set locally, including *Fernandina's Finest Easter* and *Murder in Fernandina*, which she cowrote with the Nassau County Writers and Poets Society. Her husband, Andrew, flew EMS helicopters for UF University Health Shands Hospital following his retirement from the Navy. He has been involved in local politics for many years and has donated many hours in volunteer work for various community organizations. (Courtesy Cara Curtin.)

Dave Scott
Dave Scott's career spans 45 years in journalism and corporate communications. He spent five years as a daily newspaper reporter in Florida and New York before entering corporate communications with IBM, ITT, and other Fortune 500 companies. He eventually ran his own agency. He retired to Amelia Island in 2011 and began writing a column for the *News-Leader* that has since transitioned into a popular online blog that offers updates and sharp insight into all things Fernandina Beach. (Courtesy Dave Scott.)

Dickie Anderson
Freelance writer Dickie Anderson moved to the island in 1996 and quickly established herself. "From the Porch," her weekly column in the *News-Leader*, captures Amelia Island's charm. She also writes for the *Amelia Islander* magazine and regional publications. As an active volunteer, she works with the Amelia Island Museum of History, Micah's Place, and other groups. She has served as the executive director of the Amelia Island Book Festival and has been a featured author at the event. Anderson has written several books including *Great Homes of Fernandina—Architectural Treasures from Amelia Island's Golden Age*, which profiles 25 homes in the island's historic district. (Courtesy Steve Leimberg/UnSeenImages.com.)

Stephan "Steve" Leimberg

Steve Leimberg is a man of many talents. He spent much of his career teaching tax law in Pennsylvania at the law schools of Temple University and Villanova University. He is also an expert in estate law and planning. He owns a software company that serves that industry and a subscription service that provides a weekly newsletter to attorneys. Leimberg has published books on a variety of legal subjects and regularly speaks about them as well.

Legal expertise is only the surface of Leimberg's talents. He has interests in theater and poetry and is a highly respected photographer. In 2008, he won an international photography award from Nikon for nature photography.

His interest in nature photography is tied to his love for world travel. That is what first brought him to Amelia Island by sailboat in the early 1980s. He enjoyed his visit and returned a second time. By the time a speaking engagement brought him for a third visit, he was hooked, and he and his wife, Jo-Ann, decided to make a permanent move to the island in 2008. Soon, an interest in portraits developed. That might be how he is best known locally. His "Faces of Amelia" series features portraits of many locals, including several in this book. The series has been featured around town at places like the Fernandina Beach Library. His photograph here is a self-portrait.

Leimberg has been quick to become involved in local organizations like the Wild Amelia Nature Festival, Island Art Association, and Friends of the Fernandina Beach Library. (Courtesy Steve Leimberg/UnSeenImages.com.)

Phil Scanlan

Phil Scanlan also discovered Amelia Island while on vacation. He retired from AT&T in 2000 and wasted no time in using his business experience to organize groups seeking to improve the quality of life on the island. He spearheaded the local tree ordinance and helped his neighbors establish the American Beach Community Center and Museum. In 2005, he started an initiative that ultimately brought about the development of the Amelia Island Trail that connects Peters Point with the southern tip of the island, the Timucuan Trail of Big Talbot Island, and beyond. Amelia Island Trail has a partnership with the Barnabas Center, which provides bicycles to those in need of transportation. (Courtesy Phil Scanlan.)

Mike Bowling

Vacation is also what brought Mike Bowling to town in 1993. He came from Ohio, where he had previously worked in a Ford manufacturing plant. On the heels of his invention of one of the most successful toys in history, Bowling decided to move to the ocean, and Amelia Island beat out other East Coast communities. Bowling invented the Pound Puppies in the mid-1980s. They were the top-selling toys in the world in 1986 and 1987 and were named one of *Time* magazine's top toys of the last 100 years. He continues to create new toy lines. (Courtesy Mike Bowling Enterprises Ltd.)

Cal Atwood

Cal Atwood permanently moved to Amelia Island from Atlanta in 1997. He worked in education, lecturing at places like the University of North Carolina and Emory University. He also served as a Marine during World War II and was wounded when he landed on Iwo Jima. He has made his mark in town by becoming very involved in the Amelia Island Museum of History and chairing its board. Cal is also known for his poems, which have been published in several venues. (Courtesy Steve Leimberg/ UnSeenImages.com.)

Col. Elliott "Bud" Sydnor

Col. Elliott "Bud" Sydnor was a highly decorated US Army veteran. He commanded troops in Korea and Vietnam. His most notable act was training and overseeing the ground forces involved in the Son Tay Raid that rescued prisoners of war from North Vietnam in 1970. For that, he was awarded the Distinguished Service Cross. He moved to Amelia Island following his honorable discharge in 1981 and continued to consult with the military and US government. He was inducted into the US Army Ranger Hall of Fame in 1992. Locally, Sydnor was a member of Memorial United Methodist Church and was active in American Legion Post No. 54. (Courtesy Sydnor family collection.)

INDEX

Visit us at
arcadiapublishing.com

CPSIA information can be obtained
at www.ICGtesting.com
Printed in the USA
BVHW011020051221
623268BV00003B/324

9 781540 216540